# Retirement at Risk

## KEEPING SEVEN PREDATORS AWAY FROM YOUR RETIREMENT NEST EGG

Dave Evans

Evans Financial Group
SHREVEPORT, LOUISIANA

Dave Evans/Evans Financial Group
7600 Fern Ave., Building 1200
Shreveport, LA 71105
www.evansfinancialgroup.com

Book layout ©2013 BookDesignTemplates.com

Ordering Information:
For details, contact the address above.

Retirement at Risk/ Dave Evans. — 1st ed.
ISBN-13: 978-1514892473

# Contents

**Foreword by Colin Evans** .......... 1

**Preface** .......... 5

**Predator #1 — Taxes** .......... 9

**Taxes on Social Security** .......... 10

**Defusing the IRA Tax Time Bomb** .......... 15

**Selecting the Right Advisor to Help** .......... 18

**Special Situations** .......... 20

**Why Roll Over a 401(k)?** .......... 21

**Predator #2 — Catastrophic Illness** .......... 23

**Is It Preventable?** .......... 24

**What Happens if I Get Sick?** .......... 25

**Traditional Long-Term Care Insurance** .......... 26

**Alternative Long-Term Care Insurance Solutions** .......... 28

**What About a Reverse Mortgage?** .......... 29

**Medicare and Medicaid** .......... 32

**Non-Countable Assets** .......... 35

**Annuities** .......... 36

The "Look Back" Period ........ 37

Predator #3 — Probate ........ 41

So What's the Good News? ........ 44

Keeping Up With Changes ........ 48

You Have to Fund the Trust ........ 49

Probate Horror Stories ........ 49

Famous (and Infamous) People Who Did Plan ........ 52

Predator #4 — Wall Street ........ 55

The Long Haul ........ 57

Having Time on Your Side ........ 58

NOT Having Time on Your Side ........ 58

Recovering From a Bear Market ........ 59

Wall Street's "Creative" Accounting ........ 61

Average vs. Actual Returns ........ 62

The Sequence of Returns Trap ........ 63

The Perfect Investment? ........ 66

The Truth About Annuities ........ 67

Predator #5 — Banks ........ 71

"Please, Trust Me!" .......... 72
Housing Bubble Trouble .......... 73
Who Was Watching the Watchers? .......... 74
Derivatives .......... 76
Healing the Wounds .......... 78
Trust in Tatters .......... 80
How Safe Are Banks? .......... 81
Banks vs. Insurance Companies .......... 82
The Story of Ralph and Gladys .......... 85
Predator #6 — Family and Friends .......... 89
Wrong Directions From Good People .......... 90
Money Attracts Advice .......... 91
Parentheses in Her 401(k) .......... 94
Other 401(k) Mistakes People Make .......... 95
Predator #7 — Human Nature .......... 99
Procrastination .......... 100
Getting to Know the "Why" .......... 103
Doing It Yourself .......... 105

**How to Choose the Right Advisor for YOU** .......... 107

**Ask Lots of Questions** .......... 108

**Designations and Certifications** .......... 109

**Ask Questions** .......... 110

**Other Qualifiers** .......... 113

**The Golden Rule** .......... 114

**Taking Action Is Required** .......... 115

**Afterword** .......... 117

**Acknowledgments** .......... 119

# Foreword

**by Colin Evans**

**WHEN I WAS 16 YEARS OLD, I walked into my first day of chemistry class at Captain Shreve High School in Shreveport, Louisiana. I happened to choose a seat next to a fellow student who was, like me, wearing a camouflage T-shirt and who would become my best friend. We had no way of knowing on that August day of 1993 that we would share two decades of comradery, nor could we have known the extent to which our paths would crisscross in the years to come.**

**We wound up becoming roommates at Louisiana State University in Shreveport. We waited tables together at El Chico, a Mexican restaurant on Bert Kouns Industrial Loop, a few blocks from the university. We also enjoyed duck hunting excursions, spring break camping trips at Lake Greeson in Arkansas and even a few saltwater fishing expeditions.**

**After we both graduated from LSUS, I immediately entered the financial services profession. My friend went on to pursue his dream career of law enforcement. When he was going through his police academy training, he used to practice on his roommates by**

"arresting us" until he got the procedure right. He became a law enforcement officer for the city of Shreveport and simultaneously served in the Army National Guard. As our lives went in different directions, we kept up with each other and always enjoyed having a beer or two and rehashing our "good old college days."

When my friend got married in 2005, I was a groomsman in his wedding. During the final run-through of the rehearsal at the Cathedral of St. John on Jordan Street, he was understandably nervous just before the big day. We could always tell what the other one was thinking. He nodded at me and I nodded to a few of the other guys and we all sneaked off to Bears Pub, just to have a few quick beers before the big moment.

He later became a partial client of mine. By that, I mean we only handled a small portion of his affairs. He took pride in handling most of his own financial matters. He had a life insurance policy with a $70,000 face value and his wife had an investment account of around $50,000. In the early part of 2012 he wanted to cash in his life insurance policy and help eliminate some of his wife's student loan. I remember cautioning him about canceling his coverage, but he assured me that when he re-enlisted in the National Guard, he upped his coverage through the military's life insurance program (SGLI) from $50,000 to $250,000, and that he was well-covered and felt comfortable making that change.

Sadly, in December 2012, I found myself again standing in St. John's Cathedral, this time ready to help carry out my friend's casket. Our friendship had lasted for nearly 20 years and it was a crushing, heart-wrenching moment for all of us to see his mother and wife in tears. It ripped me to the core to hear the mournful strains of TAPS played at the grave, followed by the rifle reports of the 21-gun salute. I couldn't help thinking how surreal all of it was. Three days earlier we were having lunch together.

I remember the subsequent phone calls as I helped his tearful wife through some of her financial concerns. I vividly recall the frantic tone in her voice as she told me that her husband had made a "small clerical error" when filling out his National Guard life insurance paperwork. Instead of the $250,000 he thought he was leaving behind for his young wife, the amount she stood to receive was only $50,000. This small clerical error he had made may have been inadvertent, but it would negatively affect her qualify of life in a dramatic way. Adding to the tragedy was the fact that it could have easily been prevented. I could not help but think if I had been a bit more persistent with my friend things would have turned out much differently. Had I removed my "friend hat" and put on my "professional hat" with him, I could have saved his wife a great deal of anguish.

As you read this book, written by my father, Dave Evans, I am sure you will gain much in the way of knowledge and advice. There is an old saying that "knowledge is power" and that is partially true. Knowledge is power only if you do something about it. As Napoleon Hill says in his great book, "Think and Grow Rich," "Knowledge is *potential* power." Applied knowledge is true power.

Hopefully, you are preparing to read this book to gain knowledge, some advice, perhaps some ideas or strategies for how to cope with the "what ifs" of your financial lives. The question, "What do you want to happen when what happens, happens?" is another way of saying that while we can control many aspects of our lives, there are many things that are simply beyond our control. Remember the two things in life that are unavoidable — death and taxes? That much is true. They are solid eventualities, but they are, to some extent, *manageable* eventualities. After you are gone, there will be a family meeting, perhaps in your living room, to discuss what happens next. If you have done it right, what happens next will be a pleasant occurrence for those you leave behind. If you have mishandled the opportunity to manage things, then those occurrences will not be so pleasant. Also, wouldn't it be a good idea to have a knowledgeable and qualified financial professional in that meeting, one in whom you placed your confidence and trust? My father has always said, "People don't care how much you know until they know how much you care."

The story I told you earlier is true and the name has purposely been omitted for reasons of confidentiality. The reason I relay it to you here is to explain some of the passion you will see for the points made in this book. Both my father and I have seen our share of financial mishaps and tragedies that could have been avoided, which is part of the reason why you have this book in your hand. As it was in the case of my best friend for nearly 20 years, many financial calamities can be avoided. I invite you to enjoy the book as you encounter the seven predators that could be after *your* nest egg and learn how to keep them away.

— Colin Evans

# Preface

**IF YOU BOUGHT THIS BOOK, you must be thinking about retirement. First of all, congratulations! Are you finally ready to sit back and enjoy the fruits of your labor? Great! Even if you are reading this because you want to get serious about planning for your financial future, congratulations! Your future self will thank you someday for your foresight in this regard. But a word of caution is in order. Retirement is uncharted territory that can be fraught with all manner of surprises and unexpected (and unwanted) "adventures." In the words of a couple who retired just as the 2008 market crash wiped out almost half of their retirement nest egg, "It's a jungle out there!" They are right. It can be a jungle out there — fully stocked with predators for which unprepared retirees are easy pickings. I'm sorry if that sounds scary, but I can't apologize too much because it is true! However, it doesn't have to be that way. With a little planning you can keep your financial footing throughout retirement and avoid ending up at the bottom of the food chain, so to speak.**

**What's that? You don't have a financial plan? Well, you're not alone. A 2012 study put out by Employee Benefit Research Institute**

(EBRI) revealed that 56 percent of American workers report they have not attempted to calculate how much money they will need to have saved for a comfortable retirement. Reading statistics like that is one of the reasons I decided to write this book. At the time of this writing, I have 42 years of experience behind me as a financial counselor and retirement income specialist. In that time, I have come to the conclusion that most people don't make a decision not to plan. They just don't make a conscious decision to plan. But if there ever was a need for guidance and direction in this area of life, it is now.

You wouldn't wander into the desert or trek through the jungle without a guide, would you? Nor would you set sail across the ocean without accurate charts and the latest in navigation equipment. That could be harmful to your *health.* It is just as imprudent to march into retirement without a solid financial plan. That could be harmful to your *wealth.* And yet that is what many people do. According to the EBRI, the majority of Americans have no real financial plan in place for their retirement. They simply hope "everything will work out." Hope is not a plan. You need to have a definitive course of action punctuated by specific actions, dates and dollar amounts. I am reminded of what the master of malapropisms, Yogi Berra, is reported to have said: "Be careful; if you don't know where you're going, you might not ever get there."

My primary focus is to help people who are approaching or who are in retirement plan their financial future the way a traveler embarking on a journey would map out the trip. The late, great American motivational speaker, humorist and author Zig Ziglar used to pose this question to his audiences: "Are you a wandering generality or a meaningful statistic?" It's easy to float downstream with the current and let life happen to you. It takes effort and will to take charge of your destination and maneuver through the current. As you read this book, you will come across specific strategies and concepts with which you may not be acquainted. I invite you not to dismiss these concepts out of hand because they may be unfamiliar to you. Rather, I encourage you to examine them in the light of logic and measure them by the standards of what works versus what doesn't.

In case you are wondering about the specific identity of the predators I mentioned earlier, stay tuned; we will ferret them out one by one in the chapters that follow. Some of these critters will be obvious and their danger readily apparent. Others will surprise you. Some are hiding in plain sight—well-camouflaged. Some may be no threat to you now but could appear later. It is better to know about them just in case you encounter them. Some of these predators may be easy to spot while others are hard to see unless you know what to look for. You will see what I mean. Each of these predators threatens your financial security in one way or another.

The prey/predator metaphor has made the book fun for me to write and hopefully more enjoyable and memorable for you to read. When you see taxes characterized as a jungle creature ready to pounce, it may be alarming but I assure you it is not hyperbole. When you read about what can happen to your heirs if they inherit your IRA in a lump sum (and end up giving half of it to the IRS) you will see what I mean.

You will meet the "family and friends" predator. That comparison seems like a stretch until you see what can result from following the advice of well-meaning good old Uncle Fred who loves you but has no clue what he is talking about when it comes to finances.

For some reason, the movie "Snakes on a Plane" comes to mind when I think of dangerous predators. That was one of the worst movies I ever watched halfway through, if you know what I mean. The plot was thin, the dialog was forced and the snakes were obviously computer generated images. But it made a good point—what is the worst kind of predator? One from which you can't escape.

When you're on an airplane with a slither of poisonous snakes, there's nowhere to run. Fortunately, with every predator you meet in this book, you will have an exit strategy to go with it.

I will also show you why retirees need to use caution when it comes to investing. Imagine how different the world might be today if John F. Kennedy had taken a few more precautions that fateful day in Dallas, Nov. 22, 1963. What if the Secret Service had insisted that he ride in a bubble-top convertible instead of an open car? It was discussed, you know. Was JFK too trusting, perhaps relying on the fact that it had been more than 60 years since the last president had been assassinated? Whatever the reasons, it was overconfidence and lack of precaution that took his life. Were there some in the last market crash who were caught unaware because they trusted their advisors too much? Were fortunes lost through overconfidence and failure to take proper precaution just before retirement? If so, then those attitudes, too, may be considered predatory. What was it the cartoon character Pogo is famous for saying? "We have met the enemy and he is us."

[1]

# Predator #1 — Taxes

**TAXES ARE, TO AN EXTENT, an unavoidable predator that is going to take a bite out of us regardless of what we do. The best thing we can hope to do is reduce the size of the bite. Even Jesus was resigned to that fact: "Render unto Caesar the things that are Caesar's, and to God the things that are God's." Most people don't mind paying their fair share of taxes. They just don't want to pay more than their fair share — or pay someone else's. The objective of any competent financial planner is to show you how to avoid *overpayment* of taxes.**

**There's an old joke: What is the difference between tax evasion and tax avoidance? (Drum roll, please.) About 10 to 20 years. (Rimshot, please.) But seriously folks... I have had clients tell me they are patriotic and they don't resent paying taxes. I understand the way they feel, and I applaud that sentiment. But whom do you trust more when it comes to watching over the money you have set aside for your retirement? The government or yourself? Personally, I think we can do a much better job of saving for our retirement and not wasting money than Uncle Sam.**

## Taxes on Social Security

**When you retire you get Social Security... if you are fortunate. If you are one of the burgeoning horde of baby boomers (those born between 1946 and 1964) who are stampeding into retirement at the rate of 10,000 per day, then you will most likely receive your Social Security benefits as promised. Those of you currently in your 30s and 40s may not be so lucky. Even the Social Security Administration acknowledges on their annual statements that, unless changes are made, the program will run out of money by 2034. The financial information website MarketWatch.com made the following observation about the likelihood of today's seniors receiving their Social Security[1]:**

> ***"Forecasting what will happen to Social Security is a bit different from forecasting other elements of workers' retirement plans, since, unlike 401(k)s and private pensions, the Social Security Trust Fund doesn't invest in the stock market. Uncertainty about the future of Social Security benefits is largely a political question. Balancing the system to guarantee full benefits beyond 2034 will require a reduction in benefits or an increase in taxes."***

**When President Franklin D. Roosevelt signed Social Security into law in 1935, it was to provide a form of "social insurance" during the Great Depression. This was a time in United States history when upward of 50 percent of senior citizens were living in abject poverty. Because of the market crash of 1929 and the proliferation of bank failures that followed, many saw their retirement funds disappear. Social Security was primarily designed to help take care of the elderly. The basic idea was to create a system that doled out**

---

[1] **Jeffrey B. Miller. MarketWatch.com. July 9, 2013. "Will Social Security be There for You?" http://www.marketwatch.com/story/will-social-security-be-there-for-you-2013-07-09.**

money to retirees from a fund supported by the payroll tax on current workers. The theory was that as you worked you put a few dollars from your paycheck into the system. Then when you retired it was your turn to reap the benefits, while the younger generation continued to fund the system.

The story goes that when FDR was sitting at his desk in the Oval Office of the White House, reporters asked him if Social Security benefits would ever be taxed. He is reported to have pounded his fist for emphasis and vowed, "I will never tax Social Security." This was subsequently called, so the story goes, the "Golden Promise." Whether any of that happened or not, we don't know. It's a colorful story that the Social Security Administration says is 100 percent fiction. Whether or not the story is true, FDR never taxed Social Security benefits as ordinary income for seniors. It was only after FDR *died* that Social Security benefits were taxed.

In 1983, when Ronald Reagan was president, Congress passed laws creating "tax neutrals." These sound harmless enough, right? Wrong. Tax neutrals work on the Robin Hood principle. If someone is making too much money, tax neutrals take some of that money away and give it to those earning less. This isn't exactly capitalism at its finest. In fact, this sounds like predatory behavior. In 1983, our government determined that if you were single and earning over $25,000, or married and making over $32,000, you would owe tax on 50 percent of your Social Security income.

For example, let's suppose we have a married couple, and together they receive $20,000 in Social Security income. They also have a pension that pays $15,000, and they have some 1099 income from other investments. That puts them over the $32,000 threshold, and now they will have to pay taxes on their Social Security income. Assuming that tax is going to be at a rate of about 15 percent, they will owe around $1,500 in taxes. But is it really necessary to pay that tax? Well, maybe not.

Now move the clock forward to 1993. Bill Clinton is in the White House, "grunge music" is in and Starbucks coffee is just starting to become popular. Congress passes the Omnibus Budget Reconciliation Act of 1993. One provision of this legislation increases the portion of Social Security benefits subject to taxation from 50 percent to 85 percent. The increase is designed to tax "higher income" beneficiaries. How did the government define "higher income?" If you were a single taxpayer earning more than $34,000 or married filing jointly and earning more than $44,000 as a couple, you were considered "higher income" earners and would be required to pay taxes on 85 percent of your Social Security benefits. What is that snapping sound? Is that the sound of crocodile jaws snapping shut, or a grizzly bear licking its lips? Either way, the bite of the tax predator just got bigger. But you are not helpless in this situation. There is a way out if you do a little financial planning.

The job of a competent financial advisor is to help you find ways to reduce taxation if at all possible. What if we could reposition some of that 1099 income into tax-deferred or tax-free instruments so that we could get the total income *below* the threshold? What we are dealing with is the difference between *reportable* and *non-reportable* income. If the couple in the first example had some money in certificates of deposit (CDs), for example, and those CDs earned just enough to kick them over into a taxable situation, how ironic would that be? Is the income from CDs taxable even if you never withdraw it? Absolutely! In this case, money that was never actually withdrawn could end up being counted as taxable income and amount to just enough to initiate a tax on Social Security benefits. The same could be true of gains received in a brokerage account. Even if they left the gains in the account to grow, the IRS considers that reportable income, and it could push them beyond the Social Security tax threshold. We call that "phantom income."

But what if we could slide those investments from CDs or a brokerage account to, say, U.S. government bonds, annuities or municipal bonds? Returns from those instruments are not considered taxable income in the year they were received. Annuities, for example, are "tax-deferred." You will pay taxes on it later on, down the road, when you withdraw the money. The advantage to that kind of account is the money you would have paid in taxes gets to continue working for you until you withdraw it. Do you see what I mean about the difference between letting Uncle Sam have your money and you keeping it so you can save it for your future? Let's talk about each of these three alternate investments that may help us avoid paying taxes on Social Security if it keeps us below the tax threshold.

*Municipal bonds,* as you would imagine, are issued by municipalities. Typically they are free from federal income tax and often free from state tax in the state in which they were issued. So Louisiana bonds, for example, could be federal income-tax-free and Louisiana income-tax-free. But a word of caution here. Income-tax-free is not the same as tax-free. You won't have to pay income tax on your municipal bond income, but you could still end up paying taxes on your Social Security with this instrument. How does that happen? Well, on line 8A of your income tax return you are going to have to declare how much your municipal bonds income is. You guessed it — that's going to count against you when calculating your threshold for Social Security.

*U.S. government bonds* come in many varieties. For our purpose, let say the bonds you bought for $50 mature to $100. Do you owe taxes? Not until you actually take that money out and realize a gain in income. You still need to be careful, though. Some types of government bonds pay out interest that can be *defined* as income and therefore can be counted toward your Social Security threshold. Additionally, that interest may not be taxed at the local or state level but is taxed at the federal level.

*Annuities* also come in many stripes and colors. What they have in common is that they are all issued by insurance companies and are considered to be safe investments. It's important to understand the two main types of annuities on the market — fixed and variable annuities. To use automobiles as an example, within that grouping you could say you have cars and trucks. Then, under those groupings, you have subcategories. Convertibles and sedans, dump trucks and pick-up trucks. So when you flash the word "annuity" on the screen, you may get any number of impulsive responses. But before you can form an accurate impression of annuities, you must first determine what kind of annuity you are talking about.

*Fixed annuities* come in two flavors. One pays a guaranteed interest rate that is typically slightly higher than what the banks pay on CDs. Call this one the *traditional fixed annuity.* If the bank is paying 4 percent interest, a traditional fixed annuity might pay you 5.5 percent. Again, unlike CDs, you don't pay any income tax on the interest earned by the annuity as you earn it. You only pay income tax when you actually withdraw money.

The second kind of fixed annuity is called a *fixed index annuity,* or FIA. Like all annuities, an index annuity is a contract with an insurance company for a specific period. The surrender period on an index annuity is usually about seven to 10 years. The index annuity tracks an index such as the Standard and Poor's (S&P) 500, and your return for the year is predicated on the movement of that index — thus the name. If the index goes up, you get a set percentage of the yearly return of the index from the time you deposited the money in this annuity until one year from that date, up to a pre-set maximum. These go up in value as the market goes up and when the market goes down their value is unchanged. Once you have a gain, that gain is locked in and guaranteed. This is sometimes called the ratchet/reset feature, so called because of the way a ratchet works in machinery — force is exerted in one direction but not the other. FIAs are considered safe-money investments since the principle is protected from loss. FIAs, like their traditional cousins, are tax-deferred. Your value is not subject to tax as earned income until you reach in and take it out. Index annuities typically offer a minimum guaranteed interest rate — usually between 1 percent and 3 percent, that is backed by the claims-paying ability of the issuing insurance company.

Variable annuities will be discussed more in-depth in their own section of Chapter Four, but suffice it to say that variable annuities carry a higher level of risk than their fixed cousins.

Annuities are not perfect investments for everyone, nor are they universally suitable for every investor. Like bank CDs, they come with a penalty for early withdrawal, commonly referred to as a "surrender charge." Surrender charge periods range from three to 10 years, and penalties are typically between 10–12 percent.

## Defusing the IRA Tax Time Bomb

Individual retirement accounts, or IRAs, are great for people who want a tax shelter for their retirement savings. Billions of dollars have been pumped into IRAs over the last two decades or so by persons who were seeking safety and predictability and tax-deferral. What you would have paid in taxes gets to grow in the account. That way, if you are getting a competitive rate of return, your IRA account should be able to grow into a much larger account than an account on which taxes are paid as you go. You can see why they are so popular; as long as you understand that at some future date *somebody* is going to have to pay taxes on the money that is withdrawn.

What I have seen happen in many cases is people get into retirement and view their IRA money as "last resort" money. So it never gets used. As long as it just sits there and grows, no taxes are due. Oh yes. There is this one caveat to that. The IRS requires that, whether you need the money or not, you must begin taking distributions from the IRA at age 70 ½. It's not an enormous amount and it gets bigger the older you get. It's called a required minimum distribution, or RMD. The reason it is a tax time bomb is because when the IRA owner dies and passes the account on to heirs, he or she may foolishly withdraw all of the funds, thinking that is the only option. This can create a significant tax event.

An IRA does not get a "step-up in basis" at the time of your death, not like real estate or stocks that have been owned for years and have quadrupled and quintupled in value. These are sometimes passed on to heirs upon the owner's death with no income tax whatsoever because of the "step-up in basis" rule, which allows the heirs to increase the cost basis of the inheritance upward to current market value. An IRA doesn't enjoy this tax feature. So, every dime withdrawn from an IRA is subject to income tax immediately.

Let's say a husband and wife have an IRA. The husband dies and leaves it to his wife. She rolls it over into her own IRA. Then a few years later, she dies. The money has not been touched and is now worth $250,000. She leaves it to her son, John, who earns $50,000 per year. John is in a 15 percent tax bracket. Because no prior planning was done, John is notified by the custodians of the IRA that they will be depositing a check into his account for a quarter-million dollars. The IRS considers this ordinary income that must now be taxed, not at 15 percent, but at the highest tax bracket the IRS has. John has to pay 40 percent of the $250,000 ($100,000) to the IRS in ordinary income tax! Ka-boom! The tax time bomb just exploded. But is that really necessary? Is there any way to avoid this predator? Yes, with a bit of planning.

If John's parents had made arrangements with a financial advisor or tax professional who understood Publication 590 in the IRS code, which allows for multigenerational, or "stretch" IRAs, this $250,000 could be stretched to future generations, keeping most of the money in the family for decades to come and legally disinheriting the IRS in the bargain. The money that does not go to the predatory IRS is allowed to continue growing. The distributions still come out per IRS law, but they come out based on the calculated life expectancy of younger people. Hence they are lower. Can the heirs elect to take out more if they need it? Yes. But they aren't forced to do so and pay the taxes that go with it.

All the couple who originally owned the IRA had to do was, with the help of their advisor, arrange to have specifically named beneficiaries. The IRA would be left to John and to John's children who are specifically named. There are some technical requirements that must be met for a stretch IRA to meet IRS standards. For one, the IRA must be appropriately titled. Like most documents, the wording is everything. Your financial advisor can help with this.

Also, the beneficiaries must be spelled out *just so*. Don't leave this to chance. You will need professional help here as well. Lastly, make sure your wishes are carried out by placing them in writing in your legal documents. You want your heirs to follow the instructions carefully and not accept a lump sum payout. That would nullify the stretch option and create a taxable event.

When I talk about keeping your IRA away from the tax predators, I am talking about anything that looks, feels or smells like an IRA. If you worked for the government, we might be talking about a Thrift Savings Plan (TSP) or TSA (Tax Sheltered Annuity). It could be a 501(c)(3) if you were with a non-profit organization, or a 457 plan. Whatever the shade or flavor of the IRA, it represents money you accumulated over time on which you have not had to pay

**taxes. Your goal should be to defer those taxes and avoid them as best you can.**

**Because IRAs can be inherited, most IRA owners make their spouse the primary IRA beneficiary and their children the contingent beneficiaries. Sometimes this is necessary. However, if the spouse doesn't need income from the IRA, it is a good idea to name younger beneficiaries, such as children or grandchildren as beneficiaries. Here's an example:**

**Derek has a traditional IRA valued at $500,000 on his death. If Derek's 73-year-old wife is the beneficiary, she will have to withdraw an RMD of $20,234 the next year. However, if Derek's 55-year-old son were the beneficiary, his RMD would only be $16,892. If Derek named his 28-year-old granddaughter as beneficiary, her RMD would only be $9,042 the next year. Since each beneficiary must take an RMD each year based on his or her life expectancy figure for that year, the younger the beneficiary, the smaller the RMD. That means the IRA value continues to grow by that much more and lasts that much longer. The formula will be recalculated each year using IRS Publication 590 under Appendix C – Life Expectancy Tables. Not only does passing your IRA to a child or grandchild allow the distributions to be stretched out over a much greater time span, it reduces taxes and can result in doubling or tripling the value of the IRA over time.**

## Selecting the Right Advisor to Help

**This scene appears at least once a week on television: an electronic time bomb threatens lives. Tension builds as you watch beads of sweat drip from the forehead of our hero who is bending over the device. The seconds count down. A trembling hand holds the snips and inches toward a pair of wires. Our perspiring hero goes for the red wire, then suddenly has a change of mind and goes**

for the white wire. The seconds blink to single digits. Just before the zeroes appear you hear the snick of the wire cutter. There is no explosion. The day has been saved.

You can stretch your IRA and diffuse this tax time bomb, but it is important to seek professional help — someone who understands the nuances of this strategy and can execute it properly without a hitch. Here are some things to look for:

- A firm with an underlying guarantee of between 2 percent and 3 percent over the next 150 years.
- A firm used to paying out beneficiaries that is willing to do it for the next 50-60 years.
- A firm that will administer the provisions of the contract. In other words, if you have a child in Florida, one in California and one in Pennsylvania, and you want them to get their check each year on Dec. 24, will the firm honor your wishes?
- Ideally you want a contract in advance. You want it written down that the custodian you select will carry out your wishes. Typically, only insurance companies will do all of this free of charge.

Sometimes a conversation may go like this:

*You* — "I heard about this stretch IRA strategy that can save my heirs thousands of dollars in taxes and double and triple the value of my IRA over time. Can you do that?"

*Broker* — "Stretch IRA, yeah sure I can do that." (Translation — "I don't have a clue about what you are talking about or how this works.")

Or you may hear this:

"Oh yeah, we have someone that comes in from Dallas once a year and he can do that."

Or this:

"You can do that but you have to have a trust."

That sounds to me like you are getting ready to sign up for a big attorney fee (not necessary) and you are going to pay someone to administer the terms of the beneficiary stipulations (not necessary).

There are firms that specialize in this kind of thing. Make sure you seek them out and ask questions until you are satisfied that your wishes will be carried out in the manner you intended.

## Special Situations

Let's face it: some folks just have a hole in their pockets when it comes to money. In estate planning, we refer to these individuals as "spendthrift heirs." A stretch IRA is an excellent tool if you have a beneficiary who needs your protection in that regard. If a child or grandchild does not possess the fiscal restraint to handle a lump sum, you can set up your stretch IRA to be distributed to such a relative over the course of their lifespan. This makes sure they will be provided for where it counts — a college education, for example. You can even set it up so that heirs in question will have greater control over their inheritance once they reach a milestone in their lives — such as graduation from college. The idea is that by then they will presumably "have their act together."

Another example might be an heir with special needs. In that case, you wouldn't want to restrict a child, for instance, because their medical needs are unpredictable. You can create a more flexible stretch IRA to meet the special needs of that child by allowing them to take larger distributions as needed to pay for their medical needs.

## Why Roll Over a 401(k)?

You need to be aware of something else when it comes to your retirement accounts, particularly the 401(k) from a previous employer. Some just leave their 401(k) where it is when they leave a job. This might not be the best idea for you.

One case that comes to mind involves a successful man who became very wealthy. At age 65 he was diagnosed with cancer. His wife is 62 and healthy, so she will probably outlive her husband. He made it clear that his primary concern is that she be taken care of after he is gone. When we met, he asked me to speak frankly to him. When I looked at his 401(k), I told him up front, "If you die tomorrow, the way your plan is set up, Merrill Lynch is going to write a big check to your wife. There are two problems with that. One is that she is going to be hit with a big tax bill on that lump sum payment."

"What's the other one," he asked.

"The other problem is that — human nature being what it is — she may burn through what is left."

"Like Sherman through Atlanta," he mused.

This was not what he had worked hard all of his life to have happen. I told him not to worry. We would restructure his 401(k) and turn it into an IRA. That was, when he passes away it will become her IRA, and she will not need to take any money out until sometime in the future. For sure she will not incur a huge tax bill by accepting a lump sum. It would be to the wife's advantage not to withdraw any of the funds from the IRA until she turns 70 ½. At that point, she will have to take her RMDs, but the tax bite will be miniscule.

The thing to remember is this: Every dollar in taxes that you can legally and ethically avoid paying is a dollar that you can save for your future. Taxes are one of the first places a competent financial advisor will look in an effort to preserve your assets for retirement and help make your golden years more financially secure.

[2]

# Predator #2 — Catastrophic Illness

**I SAW A BUMPER STICKER** the other day that said simply: "Life Happens."

I think the sentiment the creator of the bumper sticker was attempting to convey was that as soon as we are born we begin encountering the inevitable twists and turns of this journey we call life. In some matters, we will be able to direct our path and determine our future. In other matters, however, try as we might, we will be powerless to alter, direct or manipulate events that are bound to occur. Call it fate or call it kismet, when some things happen — you lose your wallet or catch a cold — that's life. Sometimes you are the painter and sometimes you are the canvas. Life just happens, that's all.

I mention catching a cold because that seems to be part of the human experience. The viruses that cause the common cold are out there, and I don't know of anyone who hasn't occasionally "come down," as they say, with this most common of illnesses. The only cure medical science has come up with for the common cold is —

and I know you have heard it — rest, drink plenty of liquids and give it time. Most of us just push through them until they go away.

Catastrophic illness, on the other hand, can be a real game changer. As the term suggests, a catastrophic illness is a health catastrophe, just like a hurricane, tornado or flood is a weather-related disaster. Examples would include cancer, heart attack or stroke — severe illnesses that require prolonged hospitalization and long recovery periods. These diseases usually involve high costs for hospitals, doctors and medicines, and may incapacitate the person from working, creating a severe financial hardship.

## Is It Preventable?

I recently read the book "Younger Next Year," written by Chris Crowley and Dr. Henry Lodge. Essentially, it's a book for men over age 50, showing them how they can become functionally younger every year for the next five to 10 years, and continue to live like 50-year-olds until well into their 80s. To put it succinctly, the book said to exercise and don't eat stuff that's bad for you, a way to beef up your cardiovascular system and make you a smaller target for catastrophic illness for as long as possible.

Personally, I work out at the Willis Knighton Pierremont Fitness and Wellness Center in Shreveport, Louisiana. There are four places to work out there. Downstairs, they have an indoor saltwater lap pool I use from time to time. In the equipment room, they have all kinds of fancy machines, but I usually gravitate to the treadmill, the elliptical trainer and, occasionally, the recumbent bicycle. You can go upstairs and "pump iron," an activity which I try work into the routine. Sometimes, when I am either lifting weights or running on the treadmill, people will casually ask me what my goal is. I will respond with a smile, "Trying not to die early." I say it tongue-in-cheek to elicit a laugh, but in a way I am very serious.

The fitness center where I work out is part of the WK Pierremont Health Center campus, which includes, among other medical treatment facilities, a cardiac rehabilitation unit. This facility is very close to where I go to work out. In the rehab room, there are a couple of treadmills the cardiac patients use for stress tests. When they are finished, they sometimes walk past my workout area to cool down. They are hard to miss since they must still wear the wires and a small monitor that is recording their body's reaction to the treadmill and subsequent cool down. I am telling you this to let you know what my motivation is to continue my exercise routine. I know that if I continue the activity in *this* room, perhaps I can avoid ending up in *that* room.

## What Happens if I Get Sick?

Even the best plans we lay do not prevent bad things from happening. What if we do get sick? When you retire, your health care is provided by the government with something called Medicare. Medicare is health care for people over age 65. Would it surprise you to learn that the government discriminates against you if you are on Medicare?

We had a client who was a cancer patient and was required to undergo chemotherapy and radiation treatment. He was even in the intensive care unit for a while. The bill for a portion of these services amounted to $250,000. He was 66 years old and had both Medicare and a Medicare Supplement policy. How much do you think he paid of that bill? Nothing.

When you have Medicare and the most comprehensive Medicare Supplement policy available, and you go to the hospital, it is all covered 100 percent. The Medicare Supplement policy picks up where

Medicare leaves off. Three years passed, and his cancer was in remission. His hair grew back, and his scans were indicating that he was cancer-free. All was well until he had a heart attack.

The man was diagnosed with heart disease and blockage in three main arteries. He had to undergo heart bypass surgery that cost approximately $100,000. How much did he have to pay for that? Nothing. Medicare and his Med Sup policy once again paid for everything.

So where does the discrimination come in? Medicare and Medicare Supplement policies can cover you like a glove for surgery and cancer treatment as described above. But if you have a need for rehabilitation therapy, which is considered by the government to be extended treatment or long-term care, then you may be left in financial ruin. What would have happened if the client we mentioned above had been the victim of a stroke and required extensive rehabilitation? What if he had been diagnosed with Alzheimer's disease or some other kind of dementia? How about Lou Gehrig's disease, the advanced stages of Parkinson's or multiple sclerosis? With those debilitating ailments, Medicare gives you coverage for the first 100 days. After that, Medicare coverage stops, and so do most Medicare Supplement policies. You're on your own.

So if you wonder why we list "catastrophic illness" as Predator #2, now you know. Even if you exercise and eat right, there are some things you can't prevent. Even if you have the best health insurance, you could be left in the lurch with a long-term illness. So how can you prepare?

## Traditional Long-Term Care Insurance

One way is by buying traditional long-term care insurance. Some people call this nursing home insurance. The cost of a nursing home stay varies around the country. In the Shreveport, Louisiana, area where I work and live, a nursing home will cost around $100 per day or about $3,000 per month.

When you go to buy long-term care insurance you may discover the cost is prohibitive. The older you are the more expensive it is. If you have to be medically underwritten, you must be relatively healthy in order to qualify for the insurance. It's a bit of a Catch-22. It's like auto insurance. If you have a bad driving record you either can't get car insurance or it's going to cost you a pretty penny — and you're probably the person who needs it the most.

One couple who came to our office had some challenges when it came to purchasing long-term care insurance. The woman was petite, and the husband was anything but small. In the South, he is what some would call a "big ole' boy." Unfortunately, he suffered from diabetes, high blood pressure, arthritis and morbid obesity. An insurance company would view him as a walking claim. All long-term care policies work pretty much the same way. You are a claimant if you have cognitive impairment, which can mean Alzheimer's or dementia to the point that you are not sure who you are or where you are. You are a claimant if you cannot perform two of six activities of daily living (ADLs). The six basic ADLs are eating, bathing, dressing, toileting, transferring (walking) and continence. An individual's ability to perform ADLs is important for determining what type of long-term care (e.g., nursing home care or home care) and coverage the individual needs (i.e., Medicare, Medicaid or long-term care insurance). Nearly half of all Americans who turn 65 during any given year will eventually enter a nursing home as a result of being unable to perform ADLs. The National Center for Health Studies estimates the average stay in a nursing home lasts 835 days, which is approximately two years and four months. Keep in mind this is an average. I know of some whose stay lasted only a month and others whose stay lasted more than 10 years. The wording of policies varies from one insurance company to another and

**premiums will vary according to carrier and region. I suggest you shop around or buy from an agent who represents at least five or six companies.**

**Now back to our big ole' boy. If his knees give out because of his arthritis, if his legs fail him because of his diabetes, if he discovers that he needs help getting dressed in the morning or can no longer bathe by himself, does that mean that he automatically goes into a nursing home? Not necessarily. Home health care might work. Every case is different. Perhaps he just needs someone to be there standing by and help him get dressed if he can't do it. But, as far as being able to purchase long-term care insurance, unfortunately an applicant who is overweight and beset with multiple health problems like the ones our "big ole' boy" has will be declined in the application process. So are there any other solutions besides traditional long-term care insurance?**

## Alternative Long-Term Care Insurance Solutions

**You could buy a "combo." These are products that are relatively new in the insurance world. They are called "combos" because they combine two financial products in one. The first piece is a fixed annuity that provides a guaranteed minimum return, typically of around 3 percent per year. The second piece is built-in long-term care coverage. Here's how it works: If the funds you invest are ever needed for long-term care, the amount you put in comes out first to pay for it. Then a benefit is triggered that will, in essence, provide up to *three times* the amount of the annuity for long-term care. As an example, if you purchased a $100,000 annuity and selected a benefit limit of 300 percent and a two-year long-term care benefit factor, then you would have an additional $200,000 available for long-term care expenses, even after the initial $100,000 annuity policy value was depleted. In other words, an annuity purchased with**

$100,000 could potentially pay out long-term care benefits of $300,000. That is a middle-of-the-road example, and some policies are more generous than others with offsetting trade-offs and provisions. Some companies require a physical and some don't, but there is usually some degree of underwriting. It's not for everyone, and some may object to the low rate of return. It's better than a CD, but you certainly won't get rich from 3 percent. Also, you have to put the money in all at once for it to work. But if you have no long-term care insurance at all but you have the resources, then it could be a way to go.

One of the many objections people raise about traditional long-term care insurance is that it is a use-it-or-lose-it proposition. What happens if you pay into it for 10 years and then drop the policy? Do you get any of your premiums back? No. What happens if you "die with your boots on," so to speak, and never need long-term care? Can you pass any of the premiums you paid into the program along to your family? No. With combos, you either have the return on your annuity, or you use it to pay for your long-term care. One footnote to the combos — the Pension Protection Act of 2006, a provision that became effective on Jan. 1, 2010, allows for long-term care benefits to be paid from an annuity, tax-free.

## What About a Reverse Mortgage?

If you own a home, there is an option available called a reverse mortgage. Reverse mortgages are misunderstood by many. First, let me ask you a question. If you own a home, free and clear, would you consider it an asset or a liability? Of course, most anyone would say it is an asset. But even if you have a paid-for home worth, say, $200,000, you still have some expenses associated with that property. You must still pay taxes and insurance on the home. You must also pay for its upkeep and maintenance. So, from a cash flow standpoint, money is flowing away from you. What if you could take a portion of the equity from the home and never have to pay anything back — no principal, no interest, nothing, ever — as long as you or your spouse maintain the home as a primary residence. In certain situations, a reverse mortgage may be just what you need to survive financially. Essentially, you borrow against the home's equity, and the value of the home pays back the loan. There are always fees involved when you borrow, and you need to understand what they are and why they are there. But this type of arrangement can be an attractive option for a retired person who has lots of equity built up in a home but doesn't have enough money to afford daily living expenses.

In order to do a reverse mortgage, you have to be age 62 or older and you would not enter into this type of agreement unless there is a good, solid reason for doing so. Also, please understand that you are subtracting this money from the value of your estate, so you might want to get one of those bumper stickers that says, "We are spending our children's inheritance." Someone, keep in mind, will have to pay that loan back after you are gone. Also, please be sure to work with someone who is a licensed mortgage professional to ensure you are informed of any regulations, especially those specific to your state, that may exist regarding these products.

So what am I talking about here? Buying long-term care insurance with a reverse mortgage? No. I am saying that a reverse mortgage in this situation could provide these clients with the cash flow they need to pay for a home health care provider. I'm also saying that if you need home health care and you don't have the cash to pay for it, this is one place to look. Oh, by the way — the money that comes out of your home is completely income-tax-free, and that's always a cool thing. You have the comfort of knowing that this is a Federal Housing Administration insured loan. Therefore, your heirs would never be required to pay back more than the home is worth at the time the loan is due.

> *A word of caution here: If someone ever says to you, "Hey, you take the equity out of your home, and I will help you invest it," run! They are probably not looking out for your best interest; they are probably looking out for their own. You don't do a reverse mortgage unless you absolutely need the income stream.*

I have overseen a couple of reverse mortgages for clients. I don't actually do reverse mortgages, but if it is the best solution for a client, I bring the necessary people together at no cost to the client. Also, as a fiduciary, I make sure their interests are cared for and their wishes are carried out. In one such situation, I brought in a long-term care specialist. A man and his wife who were approximately 70 years of age owned a home valued at $240,000, and they still owed about $100,000 on the existing mortgage and were paying around $1,000 per month. I suggested the couple take out a reverse mortgage and pay off the first mortgage. That way they would still have the $100,000 loan against the home, but no payments would be due until after they passed away. The interest clock would still be ticking, however, so the loan balance would continue to escalate while they were living. The couple wished to leave the property to their children upon their deaths. At that point, the heirs would have to settle the mortgage to clear the property, sell it and claim the equity, or they could refinance the mortgage into a traditional one. The primary objective here was to provide the couple with the quality of life they deserve and give them an income stream they did not have before.

## Medicare and Medicaid

Another thing that you could do assuage long-term care concerns is Medicaid planning. On the table in my office, I have articles from the Wall Street Journal, Business Week, USA Today and Money Magazine, all of which discuss some aspect of Medicaid. I also have a book that is very useful on the subject written by a man who had to find a suitable nursing home for his aging parents. It is a first-person account of all that he encountered and discovered in the process. I have studied the subject enough to know this: There is such a thing as having too much money when you are dealing with long-term health care and the government.

Because Medicaid and Medicare both start with the prefix "medi" they are often mistaken for each other. Believe me, they are two different things. Medi<u>care</u> is health care for senior adults. Medi<u>caid</u>, on the other hand, is health care, including long-term care, for the indigent — that is, people who are without money, paupers. Some people I know have a bit of a moral issue with trying to get poor to qualify for nursing home coverage. So if you feel that way, you may want to do some preparation in advance, because the government does not view Medicaid the same way it does Medicare. You must prove (and they mean business here) that you are truly impoverished before you can qualify for Medicaid. If you do go to the nursing home and you don't have long-term care insurance, you will spend all of your money first before you can be considered a candidate for Medicaid help.

Perhaps you have heard of the term, "spend down." That's when you go to a nursing home without any insurance to pay for the care, and you must begin "spending down" your resources to reach the point where you are officially a pauper in the government's eyes. At that point you then become a possible candidate for Medicaid. Whenever one spouse enters a nursing home and the other spouse remains at home, the latter is referred to in Medicaid parlance as the "community spouse."

Since Medicaid is a need-based program, there are limits on the value of assets that a Medicaid applicant and his or her spouse may own. A Medicaid applicant is usually allowed to keep only between $1,500 and $2,000 held in his or her name, after qualifying for Medicaid. There is a much higher limit on what the community spouse can keep to pay for future living expenses, but the rules on limits are very specific. When a spouse faces the need for nursing home care, the couple may wish to consider retitling assets to prepare for Medicaid eligibility.

The primary reason to retitle assets is to keep the Medicaid applicant's assets under the limit established by federal and state law. While it is true that assets in either spouse's name are considered in making the initial Medicaid eligibility determination, once the applicant qualifies for Medicaid, the spouses' assets are treated separately, based on whose name the assets are in. If you are going to go this route, it is better to transfer assets sooner rather than later. What happens if one of you becomes incapacitated and is no longer able to make the transfer? In that case, the transfer may be made only by someone authorized to make a transfer for you, such as an agent, power of attorney, conservator or court-appointed guardian. There are sometimes problems with these scenarios. Written powers of attorney may not allow for a transfer to the community spouse, especially when the community spouse is the agent. Guardianships and conservatorships are expensive and time-consuming and best avoided when possible. If the applicant is not yet incapacitated, transferring assets to the name of the community spouse will, in turn, enable the community spouse to make future transfers that may be desired or required for Medicaid eligibility.

Traditionally, married couples own their homes jointly. There may be cases where they choose to keep their ownership separate,

**such as when one spouse inherits the property, or the home was already in the name of one spouse prior to the marriage. But when a couple owns the home in both names, it may be wise to put the property in the name of the community spouse, even if the home isn't a "countable" asset when qualifying for Medicaid. First, if the Medicaid applicant/recipient becomes incapacitated, the future transfer or sale of the house may be difficult. Second, when the property is owned jointly with rights of survivorship, as many couples' houses are, if the community spouse dies before the Medicaid recipient, the house will become a countable asset of the Medicaid recipient. The Medicaid recipient may then have to sell the house to maintain eligibility if the Medicaid recipient continues to reside in a nursing home. But then, when the home does sell, the proceeds will belong to the Medicaid recipient and will disqualify the recipient from further Medicaid eligibility. Egad! That's not what you wanted to see happen!**

**Some retirement accounts present specific problems when it comes to Medicaid eligibility. Many states consider the value of retirement accounts as countable in making the Medicaid eligibility determination. And since retirement accounts can be owned only by an individual, retirement accounts in the name of the Medicaid applicant will ordinarily disqualify the applicant from Medicaid eligibility. (State laws differ about the treatment of retirement accounts, so it is crucial that you consult an elder law attorney to determine the law of your state.) Federal law does not allow ownership of a retirement account to be transferred to a spouse. So when a Medicaid applicant owns a retirement account, the only solution is to liquidate the account. Then another problem can arise. When you take money out of traditional tax-deferred retirement accounts, doing so creates a taxable event. Life insurance is not a retirement account and does not consist of tax-deferred contributions, so liquidating a life policy is one way to get the cash value.**

When you do that, however, you lose the death benefit. It may be better to simply transfer ownership of a life policy to the community spouse. That doesn't usually disqualify the Medicaid applicant since transfers to a community spouse are allowed. This way, the death benefit remains intact. The community spouse will have to maintain future premium payments to keep the policy in effect.

## Non-Countable Assets

Not all assets have to be spent or sold to qualify for Medicaid. These "non-countable" assets include the home (under $500,000 in most cases) a car, personal effects, household goods and furnishings, some prepaid funeral and burial arrangements and a limited amount of cash (generally $3,000 for a couple), to name just a few. But the determination of whether these assets are exempt, and to what extent, is made on a case-by-case basis. State laws vary on this. What if the Medicaid applicant owes money? The applicant may pay that legitimate debt if they are legally obligated. Notice the word "legitimate" here. I know of one case where the parents lived in a home that had been purchased for them by their oldest son. The elderly couple was supposed to be paying rent to the son but they had not done so and the son didn't insist they pay him, even though it was still a legitimate debt. Then the father had a debilitating stroke, and the mother was diagnosed with Alzheimer's in the same month. Both were admitted to a nursing home. The elderly couple had $40,000 in a savings account that would have gone to the nursing home had the son not kept a copy of the original lease agreement as well as a ledger of the back-due rent for several years. The auditors considered this a "legitimate" debt.

A Medicaid applicant may also pay any legitimate debt that the applicant's spouse is legally obligated to pay, for example credit cards, mortgage payments, medical bills, taxes, car payments, rent, utilities and the costs of home or car maintenance. You may even be able to pre-pay certain obligations, as in the case of mortgages and final expenses. This can be a sticky wicket because some services must actually be received before they can be paid for, like medical services and utilities. States have their own rules on this, so check with an elder law attorney first.

## Annuities

When you spend a lump sum of money on an annuity for your spouse, your spouse is guaranteed a fixed income for a specified number of years. This guarantee is backed by the financial strength and claims-paying ability of the issuing insurance company. (Your spouse's income is not counted toward Medicaid eligibility.) This could be an excellent way to spend down assets if you're married. But in order for an annuity to work as a way to spend down resources, it must meet certain requirements. For example, the annuity must be nontransferable, and your state's Medicaid agency must be listed as the primary beneficiary after the death of your spouse. You will want to speak to a financial advisor who specializes in annuities before making a decision on this.

Anytime the government is involved, you can guarantee that there will be endless complexity involved. Just one example is how much life insurance you can own and still qualify for Medicaid. If the life insurance face amount is $10,000 or below, it doesn't matter how much cash value you have. If the face amount is $10,000 and above, then the cash value will count against you and this last number comes up — which is $101,640. If all the couple's assets — and it could be cash, CDs, mutual funds, bank accounts, it doesn't matter – total up to less than $101,640, then the applicant can still qualify for Medicaid.

What happens if you have more than that? A man came to my office recently and told me that his wife was in a nursing home. He was paying $3,200 a month for her care. When all was tallied up, he had slightly less than $200,000 in investable assets over the allowable amount of $101,640. I recommended that we put this money into a Medicaid-friendly annuity. This would act just like a stretch IRA. Since he was the community spouse, he could receive approximately $1,800 per month for the rest of his life. If he died prematurely, then his heirs could get the remainder of the account. He didn't need the money, but he had a choice — take the $1,800 or pay $3,200 to the nursing home. I think this is what the kids these days call a "no brainer," which is hip lingo for an easy decision. Interestingly, there is not a limit on the income that a community spouse can have as long as it is deemed "reasonable." The $1,800 per month was deemed reasonable in this case. So we, in essence, took $200,000 in countable assets off the table, converted it into a non-countable asset, and now with his wife in the nursing home, he qualifies for Medicaid. Ideally, this kind of thing should be done in advance. Compliance must be followed to the letter of the law, and the law is complex and very specific.

## The "Look Back" Period

It used to be that people could say, "I'm just going to give my money away to my kids, and I'll tell the government that I am poor." Well, I think the government got wise to that and tightened the rules. They instituted "look back" periods and denied transfers of assets just to qualify. These looks back are different in length and in severity of the penalty, depending on when the gift or transfer was made.

- For gifts or transfers made *before* Feb. 8, 2006, the look back period is 36 months (three years) from the date of the Medicaid application. If a gift or transfer for less than full value falls within this time, then the period of ineligibility begins to run from the date of the transfer.

- For gifts or transfers made on or *after* Feb. 8, 2006, the look back period is 60 months (five years) from the date of the Medicaid application. And if a less-than-full-value transfer falls within this time, the period of ineligibility begins from the date of the application for Medicaid coverage (NOT from the date of the transfer, as under the earlier rule).

I have a personal story for you. My mother-in-law lives in New Jersey. When my father-in-law was alive they had been in the rental property business, and they sold their rental property and they said, "Dave help us, what should we do with our money?" So I helped them develop a plan. I wrote them a letter and told them to stagger some CDs, draw on the money a little bit at a time, and this should last them until around age 85. They are 20 years my senior. I also told them in the letter that if they ran out of money I would take care of them. I meant that from the bottom of my heart and still do.

Later on, when my beloved in-laws paid a visit, my father-in-law says, "Dave I still have that letter — the one that says you were going to take care of us when we get old." I honestly couldn't remember what he was talking about at first.

"You know, we sold those rental properties and we have just been spending the money like a drunken sailor because you said you would take care of us." His smile and the twinkle in his eye told me that I was being ribbed in his typical, good-natured way. When he died a few years later, my mother-in-law, who is now also deceased, was 77. At the time of her husband's death, she was in excellent health and played golf every day.

When my wife, Gale, was ready to take the 1,500-mile trip to see her mother, she asked me if I wanted her to convey anything to her. I told her that we needed to discuss long-term care with her at some point. There was the distance to be considered, and I wanted to understand her wishes regarding long-term care just in case. Having accrued much experience with this subject over the years, I understood that this was a possibility. After all, it is estimated that almost 50 percent of all Americans over 65 will spend some time in the nursing home before they die.[2] But I knew it would not be an easy subject to broach with my mother-in-law, and I was right!

"I'm not going to go into any nursing home," she protested. "I will just kill myself."

The pert octogenarian was joking, of course. Wasn't she? It may have been said in jest, but there was an undercurrent there that conveyed a deep concern she had, the concern of many seniors of advanced age — losing their sense of control and forfeiting their independence. I told her that she couldn't kill herself; it was against the law.

"I'll have the neighbors do it then," she snapped back. It was good natured, just like the ribbing I had received from her husband. But I began to see how strongly she felt. It explained for me why many people don't plan for this eventuality. They don't want to think about it. They postpone making any plans. If they ignore it, maybe it will go away. Also, I think I understand what happens when family members try to step in and make those plans. It can be an emotional discussion no one wants to have, so it gets tabled for "later on," which is often too late.

The ostrich has a reputation for doing something like that, but it's a bad rap. It may *appear* as if the ostrich is sticking its head in the sand to hide from danger, but that is not the case. This large, flightless bird has a much more intelligent and useful evasion tactic

---

[2] Linda Lawson. Baptist Press. "Almost Half of Americans Over 65 Will Spend Time in a Nursing Home." March 27, 2000.

at its disposal — it can run as fast as a horse! But myths are hard to unseat once they become embedded.

When it comes to the subject of long-term care, many humans tend to stick their heads metaphorically in the sand. They think that if they ignore the problem — the likelihood they will need long-term care — maybe it will go away. We all know better. Here are a few statistics compiled in 2012 by Morningstar, an independent research firm:

- If you are just now turning 65, you have a 50 percent chance of spending at least some time in a nursing home.
- There is a 68 percent probability a person over age 65 will become cognitively impaired or unable to complete at least two "activities of daily living" — including dressing, bathing or eating — over his or her lifetime.
- The median annual rate for nursing-home care in the U.S. is $73,000 and increases an average of 3.63 percent per year.
- The average length of stay in a nursing home is 2.44 years.

The math is stark. Ignoring this predator just makes the bite worse if it does get you. The thing to do is visit a financial professional who can acquaint you with your options in full detail as soon as possible. That's the best way to avoid becoming prey to an unfortunate situation later on in life.[3]

[3] Christine Benz. Morningstar. Aug. 9, 2012. "40 Must-Know Statistics About Long-Term Care."
http://news.morningstar.com/articlenet/article.aspx?id=564139.

# [3]

# Predator #3 — Probate

**THE THIRD PREDATOR IS PROBATE.** The word "probate" comes from the Latin word "probatum" which essentially means "a thing proved." We only use it nowadays to refer to the legal process by which we pass on things of value to other people when we die. The stated purpose of the probate process is to "officially prove a will" to the courts and all who would have an interest in what we leave to whom when we pass away.

Why is probate a predator?

1. Cost — One reason is that the process has become more and more complicated over the years. If you are involved in the process, perhaps as an heir or the next of kin, probate will cost you money. You are going to meet some people you have never met before — a probate attorney, a probate judge and an accountant or an appraiser, just to name a few. Legal fees, executor fees and other costs must be paid before your assets can be fully distributed to your heirs. Where's the money going to come from? Your estate! If you own property in other states, your family could face multiple probates, each one according to the laws of that state. These costs can

vary widely, too. There is no national menu of costs associated with this process. It seems as if each state makes up its rules.

2. Time consuming — Probate is a thief of time and the period between when the will is filed in court and when the funds and property are distributed can be unreasonably long.

Louisiana, the state where I work and live, is roughly in the shape of a boot walking west. I live in Shreveport, which is at the top of the toe, just southeast of the junction where Texas, Arkansas and Louisiana meet. Typically in Louisiana, it takes around nine months for a *simple* estate to go through the probate process.

From time to time, I sponsor free educational workshops on estate planning and retirement readiness and the subject of probate often comes up. It seems everybody has a story, and none of them is pleasant. One woman who came to a workshop told me her husband had died six years ago, and she still had not settled his estate because of a lengthy and complicated probate process.

Another woman told me that she had inherited money from her brother. She was the only heir to an estate, and she was the executor. There were no claims against the estate and no complications she could identify. She had a lawyer, but she still did not have the money after two years of waiting. I told her she needed a new lawyer and that it could still take some time.

During probate, assets of the estate are frozen. Ostensibly, this is so accountants and appraisers (all of whom charge fees) can make an accurate inventory. A judge can and often will deny a family of money it needs to live on after the breadwinner dies. This is not because the judge is hard-hearted. He must obey the law, and the law stipulates that probate has precedence over need.

3. Public — Probate is a public record. That means everybody and his second cousin's uncle can see what your loved one put in his or her will. I once had a client who asked me if I could accompany her downtown to the courthouse because her ex-husband's uncle

had died, and she thought he might have left her son some money in his will. Did you know that you can go right down to the Caddo Parish courthouse and look at the wills that were probated last week and see who left what to whom? It is public record. It's all right there for anyone to see.

The probate process, by law, actually invites any "interested party" to come and see what you owned, whom you owed and who will receive your assets. Along the way, any disgruntled heirs can come to contest the will and expose your family to unscrupulous solicitors. In case you are wondering why such personal matters can be made so public, the answer lies in the wording of the Freedom of Information Act. This legislation makes all information held by the government that is not related to issues of national security a matter of public record. Documents held by the courts, which is a branch of the government, may be assessable and copies of them may be made. This includes land and estate documents such as wills.

Embarrassment and the loss of privacy aside, the biggest danger here is the fact that predators search probate filings like wolves after prey. Horror stories exist of unscrupulous people who prey on young people who inherit money. Where no trust is in place, or other adequate protections, any money or insurance benefits left to children who have lost their parents will transfer to them outright at the age of 18. How many 18-year-olds do you know who would make wise decisions with a lump sum of money? Also, con artists may lurk nearby after such an inheritance to help inexperienced heirs make those unwise decisions with their new wealth.

4. It is contestable — Probate opens a will to the scrutiny of those who would contest its provisions. Would it bother you if, after your death, your assets were not distributed to your heirs in the manner you intended? When contests over an estate erupt, it is usually not a pretty sight. Family feuds over inheritance after a death in the fam-

**ily are almost proverbial. Just think about all the family members who could be unpleasantly surprised after the death of a loved one. There's the disgruntled daughter who inherits not one piece of the family china. Then there's the unhappy son who gets a smaller share of the estate than his sister, who he suspects was always the favorite. What about the niece who wasn't even mentioned in the will? It happens all the time. Are these people just being greedy? Not necessarily. Perhaps they are just emotional. Or they may be hurt and confused, which leads to suspicion, anger, resentment and hostility.**

**"Dad liked me best. He told me repeatedly over the years that he wanted me to have the GM stock and the beach house."**

**Remember the woman who said she had been waiting six years for her estate to be settled? Guess what the problem was? Squabbles between warring family members of the deceased over property. Care to guess who is paying for that squabble? The estate of the deceased. It is being drained with every passing day the probate process continues.**

## So What's the Good News?

**The good news is that all of these evils can be significantly reduced and avoided altogether with a little estate planning. The good news is that your loved ones, with a little planning, will be able to grieve and mourn your passing without worrying about court proceedings and without watching your estate be whittled away by the evils of the probate process. Most people are unaware they can avoid probate, which is why so many fail to do so. We will explore some of the ways to avoid probate. What will work in your situation may not work in someone else's. It all depends on how your assets are titled and what you want to do with them. Strategies to probate-proof your estate include:**

**TRUSTS — One way, and probably the most extreme, to avoid the probate of your estate is simply to get rid of all of your property. Wait a minute… it's not what you think. That's essentially what a trust does. In certain cases "giving away" most of your assets through the use of a particular type of trust of which you can be the beneficiary may make sense. A revocable living trust, for example, is a written agreement that covers three phases of your life:**

- **While you are alive and well**
- **If you become mentally incapacitated**
- **After you die**

**But having a revocable living trust agreement is not enough, by itself, to avoid the probate of your property after you die. Your trust *must own your assets* in order for them to be probate-proof. We call this "funding the trust." Try to visualize your trust as an empty bucket, which you may fill with your assets in order to ensure those assets will avoid probate after you die. If any of your assets are outside the trust when you die, these "unfunded assets" will need to be probated. Trusts trump wills, no matter how specifically a will is worded. A knowledgeable estate attorney will know how these documents need to be set up in order to properly protect your estate.**

**Another thing that you can do to avoid the probate process is you can set up something called a *living trust*. This is going to cost around $2,000, and I suggest you don't try to do it over the Internet or pay $800 to a cheap lawyer who operates by mail in another state just to save a few bucks. Trying to save a few hundred dollars can cost you thousands of dollars down the road. In Louisiana, the state where I work and live, there are rules that stipulate such documents must be prepared by an attorney who practices law. An excellent reference on trusts is "The Bible of Living Trust, How to Avoid Probate," written by Henry Epps, an attorney.**

**DESIGNATED BENEFICIARIES — One of the first things I do with new clients is a document review. One of the most important lines of a life insurance policy, an annuity or an IRA is the line where you designate a beneficiary. In general, documents with designated beneficiaries are probate-proof. Whoever you list as your beneficiary on a document such as the ones mentioned above is the individual, or individuals, to whom the proceeds of the policy or account will go in the event of your death. If it sounds like I am stating the obvious, I apologize. I cannot tell you how many times I have looked at a statement or a policy during document reviews and seen either no beneficiary listed (particularly this is the case with IRAs and annuities) or the beneficiary designation is out of date.**

**I recommend that you have two beneficiaries for each document, a primary and a contingent beneficiary. In a typical husband/wife situation, the surviving spouse will be the primary beneficiary and the children will be the secondary, or contingent, beneficiaries. Whom you select is up to you, of course.**

**What's wrong with this picture — a life insurance policy with the word "spouse" on the beneficiary line? Everything! What happens if your spouse predeceases you, or you happen to both die in a car accident? Will the kids eventually receive the proceeds from the policy? Most probably, but how do you feel about them receiving it nine months to two years after your death? That is so unnecessary. When I see the word "spouse" on the beneficiary line, I know that a lazy insurance salesperson just didn't bother to ask questions and structure the policy in the client's best interest. I have seen documents where the beneficiary line was cramped, and there was little room to write. That's OK. Use a separate sheet of paper to list *exactly* how you wish the proceeds of the policy or the account to be distributed. Use as much ink as you need. Spell out percentages if you wish. In the event of your death, those who are called upon to disburse the funds are required by law to abide by your wishes.**

Would it surprise you to learn that in some cases an annuity will show the *writing agent* as the beneficiary? As bizarre as that may sound, I have seen it several times. Annuity companies may require a Change of Beneficiary form. You can quickly download these, enter the correct information, sign them and either email them or fax them back to the issuing insurance company in a matter of minutes.

Some are not aware that insurance companies don't write checks to little kids. During one document review, I noticed a couple had an insurance policy with the name of their son, age 10, listed as the primary beneficiary. The man had been married before, and his current wife was sitting beside him.

"Who would be taking care of 10-year-old Tommy if you were to die?" I asked.

"His real mother, my ex-wife," he replied.

"You do understand that the insurance company will not make a check out to your son, don't you?" I continued. "Your ex-wife will get the money. That's OK with me if that's OK with you."

He was immediately shaking his head "no" as his wife's eyes opened wider in amazement. There was a story here, I knew. Perhaps one with some unpleasant history. But I didn't ask.

JOINT OWNERSHIP WITH RIGHTS OF SURVIVORSHIP — When you add joint ownership to a property, it goes a long way to settling any dispute about who should own the property after your death. Obviously, it's the person whose name appears opposite yours on the title, deed or ownership document. Take bank accounts, for example. Adding another name (a spouse, for example) as a joint owner to a bank account will usually avoid probate. The same goes for an investment account or to the deed for real estate. It must be made clear on the document that the account is owned by joint tenants with the rights of survivorship and not as tenants in common. A word of caution: don't rely on joint ownership with rights of survivorship or tenancy *alone* to avoid probate. Each state

**has its own laws, and there may be wrinkles in joint ownership that a competent estate attorney will be able to iron right out.**

**The bottom line is this: There are several strategies that may help you avoid probate. It will depend on your unique family and financial circumstances which ones will work for you. I suggest you open the dialog as soon as possible. Planning has to take place *before* the event that you are planning for takes place. It will likely be a difficult time for the family. Proper planning creates peace of mind for all of them.**

## Keeping Up With Changes

**A great deal of my time as a financial professional is spent keeping up to date on changes in the law as it pertains to wealth management. The Homestead Exemption was put in place by Louisiana voters in 1980 at $75,000. Under the Article VII, Section 20 of the state constitution, only one Homestead Exemption can be granted per home that is owned and permanently occupied by a resident in Louisiana. A Homestead Exemption cannot be applied to a property that an individual owns but does not live in day-to-day. In other words, you can't live in Atlanta and get a Homestead Exemption for a home in Orleans Parish. The exemption means $75,000 that you don't have to pay taxes on. A few years ago, if you put your home in a living trust, you lost your homestead exemption. You would realize that if you placed the property in the Homestead Exemption and subsequently saw your tax bill go up. It happened to a lot of folks. They would take it back out of the trust to fix the problem.**

**What's that got to do with the price of tea in China? Trusts can be drafted as *revocable* (or modifiable) or *irrevocable* (or unmodifiable) trusts. When Amendment 11 was placed on the ballot in 2006, and voters approved it, then you could claim your Homestead Exemption if your home was placed in a *revocable* trust. You didn't**

**have to lose your $75,000 exemption if you wanted to protect your house from the probate process.**

**Trusts are wonderful things. You can literally put all of your assets in a trust, and you no longer own them! The trust owns them! You own the trust, but, when you die, nothing in the trust is going to go through the probate process. Essentially, it says that if you die, your wife gets it, or if she dies, then the kids get it, or the grandkids get it... You get the idea. It is a smooth transition.**

## You Have to Fund the Trust

**Sometimes I have people who come into my office and want me to look at their trust. They give me a three-ring binder that weighs 10 pounds and cost them $2,000. After wading through the legalese (a necessary evil) of the document, I will ask them, "What do you have in the trust. I don't see anything listed here."**

**"Oh, we haven't put anything in it."**

**I tell them that until they fund the trust, or actually list the assets they want protected, all they have is a $2,000 three-ring binder. It's a waste of time and money if you have a trust drawn up and don't transfer assets to it.**

## Probate Horror Stories

### Anna Nicole Smith

**The case of Anna Nicole Smith will have to go down as one of the strangest, most convoluted and long-lasting estate messes in the history of probate court. It has become the estate fight that refuses to die. The former Playboy Playmate, stripper and reality TV star (whose real name is Vickie Lynn Marshall, by the way) became the wife of 89-year-old Texas oil billionaire, J. Howard Marshall. At**

this writing, litigation has been ongoing for 18 years with no end in sight. Millions of dollars have been spent so far on legal fees. It has seen two trips to the United States Supreme Court so far, and the case lives on.

She married Marshall in 1994. The case began 14 months later when the oil tycoon died and left her out of the will, leaving everything to one of his sons, Pierce Marshall, instead. The probate proceedings started in Louisiana and then moved to Texas. Pierce Marshall died at the age of 67 in June 2006, leaving his heirs to continue fighting for the $1.6 billion estate. Anna Nicole Smith died Feb. 8, 2007, from an accidental drug overdose, but not before a California judge awarded her $475 million — money she would never see. Even if the Smith estate wins its latest appeal, observers of the bizarre legal battle say legal fees will be so much that Smith's young daughter, Dannielynn Marshall, may never see a cent. That's what can happen when an 89-year-old billionaire falls in love with a woman one-fourth his age.[4]

## Marilyn Monroe

One of the most egregious examples of how failure to plan properly can cost your heirs is the estate of 1950s blonde bombshell Marilyn Monroe. She was a global symbol of beauty and glamor when she died on Aug. 5, 1962. Now, more than 50 years later, she (her estate that is) is making more money than Miss Monroe ever dreamed of. Her image appears everywhere these days — on posters, T-shirts, coffee mugs and refrigerator magnets. The beauty icon would roll over in her grave if she knew where the multiple millions in royalties are going. Monroe did have a will, but she left the bulk of her estate to her acting coach, Lee Strasberg. He and his

---

[4] Michelle Fabio. LegalZoom. Dec. 2009 "The Legal Mess Left Behind by Anna Nicole Smith." https://www.legalzoom.com/articles/the-legal-mess-left-behind-by-anna-nicole-smith.

**wife, Paula, were like surrogate parents to Monroe. Strasberg died in 1982, his second wife, Anna, who had no connection to Monroe, inherited the estate. Anna Strasberg licenses all the Monroe products and memorabilia through a company that specializes in managing the estates of dead celebrities.**

## Other Celebrities Who Failed to Plan

**Other rich and famous folks who failed to plan include:**

***James Dean,* who died when he was 29 in a car crash and didn't have a will. His entire estate, including the licensing fees that still generate $1 million to $3 million annually, defaulted to his next of kin. In Dean's case, his closest living relative was his estranged father, who had abandoned Dean and his family as a child.**

***John Denver,* who died in a plane crash in 1997. Denver left no estate plan for his $19 million estate, and failed to name a beneficiary on his pension. As a result, probate for the estate and IRS tax disputes took more than six years. The pension lost tens of millions of dollars in taxes (not to mention potential tax-free compounding) that could have gone to Denver's children.**

***F.W. Woolworth,* founder of the Woolworth's retail chain, who left his estate to Barbara Hutton, his granddaughter. Hutton inherited the $25 million trust from her grandfather when she was 10 years old. The trust ended when Hutton turned 21 in 1933, effectively handing her about $50 million dollars in the early years of the Great Depression. Hutton died at age 66 with $3,000 to her name, on the verge of bankruptcy, after seven husbands, years of spousal abuse, drug addiction, uncontrolled spending and exploitation.**[5]

---

[5] **Steven M. Greenwood. "People You Know Who Didn't Plan." http://www.caestatelaw.com/people-you-know-who-didnt-plan/.**

## Famous (and Infamous) People Who Did Plan

### O.J. Simpson

**A name that will probably live in infamy is that of former NFL football star O.J. Simpson. In one of the most well-publicized court cases of our times, he was acquitted of the murder of his wife, Nicole Brown Simpson, and her friend, Ronald Goldman. However, when the Brown and Goldman families pursued a civil suit against him, Simpson's ample estate was at risk. Despite the ex-footballer's alleged misdeeds, one thing he did right was to put good asset protection planning in place. When the civil suit progressed, Simpson's defined-benefit retirement plan (valued at more than $4 million) was "off limits." In other words, the judge presiding over the civil case ruled that Simpson's retirement plan could not be used as a source of proceeds to satisfy the judgment won by the Brown and Goldman families. If you ever wondered how Simpson was able to play golf and live easy for all those years after the civil courts supposedly stripped him of everything he owned, the answer has to do with the federal laws that protect creditors from touching retirement programs. In 1997, Goldman's parents and estate, along with Nicole Brown Simpson's estate, were awarded $33.5 million in judgments after a civil jury found Simpson liable for the deaths, but the money has gone largely unpaid because his money was in his NFL pension and an annuity, both of which are probate-proof and beyond the reach of creditors. At this writing, "The Juice" is serving time in a Nevada prison for kidnapping, assault and his involvement in a Las Vegas robbery. He has reportedly asked for President Barack Obama to pardon him since he doesn't have much longer to live.**[6]

---

[6] **MW Patton. Jan. 14, 2013. "What OJ Simpson Can Teach Us About Domestic Asset Protection." http://www.mwpatton.com/asset-protection-articles/oj-simpson-teach-domestic-asset-protection/.**

## Babe Ruth

Babe Ruth grew up in an institution for underprivileged boys and went on to become a baseball legend and a loved national celebrity in the 1920s and 1930s. It was a time when most professional baseball players earned very little, but the "Sultan of Swat" was an exception. In 1930, the New York Yankees paid Ruth an astounding (at the time) $80,000 to play for them. Remember, this was during the Great Depression. Most players were struggling just to make ends meet, and Ruth lived a life of luxury compared to them.[7] The "Sultan of Swat" became famous for his charitable deeds; he once promised to hit a home run for a boy who was in the hospital. He appeared to be careless with money, but he bought several annuities from Harry Heilmann, a friend who played for the Detroit Tigers and sold insurance in the offseason. This was perhaps the smartest move Ruth ever made. As Ruth aged and his baseball skills waned, the annuities he had purchased from 1923 to 1929 enabled him to keep living a luxurious lifestyle even as others were barely getting by.[8]

We could go on and on with stories about celebrities who planned poorly (or didn't plan at all) and those who planned well. Sadly, the former outnumber the latter by a considerable margin. It does not have to be that way with you.

---

[7] Graham Womack. Hardball Times. April 2, 2013. "How Hall of Famers rank for salary in 2012 dollars." http://www.hardballtimes.com/how-hall-of-famers-rank-for-salary-in-2012-dollars/.

[8] Marshall Smelser. "The Life That Ruth Built." 1975. Page 258.

[4]

# Predator #4 — Wall Street

**YOU WAKE UP.** It's a perfectly fine day outside. The sun is shining, and the birds are singing. You feel good. You wave at the neighbors as you buckle your seatbelt and head for the office. They wave back. All is ordinary and going according to plan when suddenly, halfway across the world, a bomb goes off in front of a building, or some European country is in the news for devaluing its currency or defaulting on some international loan. The next thing you know the stock market is plunging like a stone. You scramble for the screen that displays your portfolio, only to find out your account is leaking badly and listing to port. What should you do? Sell? Stand pat? Hold on? Buy? You call your broker and get the voice recording. "This is my life's savings we are talking about here!" you yell at the computer screen. "Why didn't somebody warn me this could happen?"

Will Rogers put it this way: "To make money, buy some good stock, hold it until it goes up, and then sell it. *If it doesn't go up then don't buy it.*"[9] I will give you some time to think about that one.

The cowboy philosopher also is reported to have said, "You know, when someone is talking to me about my investments, I'm not so much as concerned about the return *on* my money as I concerned about the return *of* my money." The famous American humorist and social commentator died in 1935, but his words, which are truer now than they were then, were ahead of their time.

Or how about this one? You lost money in the 2001-2002 market crash, and you are talking to your broker and he says: "What are you worried about; it's a *paper* loss." And he is right! It was a paper loss. Dollars are paper, aren't they? And that's what you lost!

If Will Rogers were alive today he would probably have something to say about "paper losses." If it is only a paper *loss,* then two years previously when the stock market knew only one direction — up — and we were making 30 percent gains, were those only paper *gains?*

If you had bought into the stock market when it peaked in September 1929, the Dow Jones Industrial Average would have been at 381.17. Then you would have looked on in horror as the market collapsed, falling to a low of 40.56 on July 8, 1932. Every $100.00 invested, peak-to-trough, became $10.64 as the national economy spiraled downward. It would not be until 25 years later, on Nov. 24, 1954, that the stock market would make it back to the perch from which it descended. That's the tricky thing about Wall Street. It does come back, but it may take a while.

Those who are retired or on the cusp of retiring don't have "a while" to wait.

---

[9] Donald H. Gold. Investor's Business Daily. "How to Invest: Buy High, Not Low, Then Sell Higher." http://education.investors.com/investors-corner/605244-disbelieve-buy-low-sell-high-myth.htm.

One couple sat in my office with expressions that were next to tearful. They had just lost half their life savings in the stock market crash of 2008. They had planned to retire in three years, and now that was going to be impossible.

"Our broker told us to just 'hang in there,'" sniffed the woman, "it will all come back."

"Yeah," continued the man. "He told us that we were not alone. He said that when the tide goes out, all the boats go down with it. When the tide comes back in, all the boats will rise."

"That was supposed to be a consolation," the woman huffed. "I was raised on the coast. I think I know a thing or two about tides. That's true, all the boats do go up and down with the ebb and flow of the tides. But in this case, *the entire ocean left!*"

## The Long Haul

Another pat expression stock brokers like to use when the market sours goes like this: "Look, this is an investment. You *are* in it for the *long haul,* aren't you?"

I don't want to hurt anybody's feelings here, but you don't need to be buying green bananas if you are approaching retirement age. The long haul is not as long as it used to be if you catch my drift. If you are at or near retirement age, there are certain things that are not what they used to be. Perhaps you are thinking about your eyesight, your weight, your drives off the tee or your agility on the tennis court. As a financial guy, I was thinking more about your time to recover financially after a stock market downturn.

## Having Time on Your Side

**You can do no wrong if you are a young investor — especially if you invest on a regular basis. Remember when they called that office meeting and told you that the company was going to sponsor something called a 401(k)? You could put a part of your paycheck into it each week, and the company would match what you put in up to a certain percentage of your salary. And the best part of all, you didn't pay any taxes on what you put in! Sweet deal! There was a maximum you could put in, right? So, if you were smart, you put in the maximum. That way the company had to match it. It was like free money!**

**Then Vanguard or Fidelity or another one of those big companies would take your contribution and invest it in stock market mutual funds. If the stock market went up, that was wonderful — your account grew in value. If the stock market went down — fantastic! Why? Because then the shares were cheaper. Your contribution bought more of them. You didn't worry. When the market finally went up again, your skinny shares would plump up, and your account would grow that much more. You were protected by this magnificent force field called *dollar cost averaging.***

## NOT Having Time on Your Side

**That wonderful dollar cost averaging force field turns into its evil twin, *reverse dollar cost averaging,* when you get older. The difference is time. Here you are in full retirement. When you stopped working, you stopped contributing to that tax-deferred 401(k) program. Now the money river is flowing in reverse. Instead of putting money into that retirement fund, now you must withdraw from it to meet expenses and enjoy life. That's why you saved it. It is a retirement account, after all. But those withdrawals**

**are made with the same regularity as your earlier deposits were made — every week, every week, every week (or month). Only now, the withdrawals are much more than the contributions. You have to cover that missing paycheck, and in order to do so, you must now *sell* shares of stock in those mutual funds. If the price of shares fluctuates (which they always will) you still have to write yourself the same paycheck, don't you? If share prices go up, you sell *fewer* shares to get the same amount. If share prices go down you sell *more* shares to make the same paycheck. If a market crash occurs, the value of your account goes down dramatically. Those losses are not paper losses. They are real. When you were working, dollar cost averaging would be snapping up cheaper shares when the market fell, but not now.**

**You've heard of compound interest, right? It's great when you're getting it but painful if you are paying it. Same principle here. To make matters worse, you are depleting the account at a faster rate. Every share you sell is one less share that will be working for you in the account.**

**That's why one of the first things you should do when you quit working and retire is to move that 401(k) into an IRA. I call it "moving it out of harm's way."**

## Recovering From a Bear Market

**The animal kingdom is full of creatures that will lull you into a sense of complacency with their cuteness and then kill you. The hippopotamus is one of the most unpredictable beasts on the planet. These slow-moving behemoths look so tame, waddling around their muddy wading pools. You almost get the urge to see if you could ride one. Cartoon artists love hippos. We probably can't get the image of hippos wearing tutus as projected in the Disney cartoons out of our minds. But these hippos are extremely territorial**

and aggressive. They can run faster than a human for short distances. They have teeth the size of bowling pins and, according to National Geographic, they kill more humans per year than any other animal in Africa. The reason they are so fearsome is because they are unpredictable. One minute they may let you wander through their herd unscathed. The next minute they will charge you without provocation. And get this... they are herbivores... plant eaters![10]

There are those who believe they can predict the stock market. They squint at their charts and study every little tick up and down and analyze this movement with a view to telling you what the market will do next. The airwaves are choked with TV analysts who come on and make exhaustive and elaborate prognostications as to which way the market will go. Horse feathers! It may sound like heresy to those who practice statistical analysis, but no one can predict the future of the market. They can only read its past and make slightly more educated guesses than a third-grader. If any of them could predict the market, they should be shot for not telling us about the crashes before they occur.

That doesn't mean we can't learn from the past. Indeed, we can! The past is a great indicator of how we should respond to the market's unpredictability. One thing we learn from looking at the past is that the market has cycles. Bull market cycles and bear market cycles.

Wouldn't it be great if we could see into the future, invest long during the bull markets, and sell short when a bear market rolls around? Of course! Averages can be tricky. They do not tell the whole story. Put one hand in cold water and the other one in hot water, on average you are comfortable. So, just because the average

---

[10] Anouk Zijlma. GoAfrica, About.com. "The Hippopotamus." http://goafrica.about.com/b/2006/11/18/the-hippopotamus.htm.

recovery time is five years doesn't mean they can't be much longer. The recovery time from the Great Depression after the 1929 market crash was 25 years!

On the other hand, some bear markets have been very brief but quite severe. Take the 1987 crash, for example. That little recession only lasted three months. Some recessions have been very brief but very deep. Remember 1987? That little downturn lasted only three months, but the S&P lost a whopping 33.5 percent! The recovery period was about two years.

The next bear market lasted from March 2000 to October 2002. The S&P went down 49.1 percent! That one lasted 31 months, and it took investors 87 months (more than seven years) to regain what they lost.

If stock market crashes could be given names the way they name hurricanes, then the one that began on Sept. 29, 2008, was our Katrina. Several of us stood numbly by in the office and watched as that little crawler at the bottom of the television screen announced that the Dow had lost 777 points that day. That was a record for a single day. Officially, the bear market began in October 2007 and continued through March 2009 — around a year and a half. But investors had never seen the likes of this before. The last economic storm to hit this hard was the Great Depression. Overall, the S&P lost 56.7 percent!

## Wall Street's "Creative" Accounting

With retirees and those approaching retirement, the primary goal is to preserve assets and protect them from loss. If we can do that and still carve out some good, solid growth then it is "mission accomplished" for most of us. One way to get there is to understand what we are looking at when we look at the "growth opportunity" that those who deal strictly with market-based portfolio management are selling. Let me show you the way Wall Street calculates a regular term on your favorite mutual fund, for example.

If you went to the mutual fund marketers in 1999, told them to put you in something risky and gave them $9,000 to play with, what do you think they would have done? They would have told you about the technology sector. They would have pointed out that these mutual funds are red hot and are going to do really well this year. And you know what? They would have been right! They were red hot! They did go up — 100 percent or more — that year! Uncork the champagne and let the confetti drop! Paint smiley faces on your mailbox and sing "Happy Days Are Here Again."

As 2000 rolls around, you now have $18,000 in your mutual fund account, and you are feeling pretty perky! However, things turned sour in a hurry when the tech bubble began leaking air, and by April 2000, the technology sector was sinking like a stone, losing half of its value. Now you are back down to the $9,000 you started with.

So, what was the rate of return from point A to point B? Zero, right? You started with $9,000 and two years later you have $9,000. That's easy. But that's not the way the mutual fund industry calculates a rate of return. They say it went up 100 percent then lost 50 percent, that's a net of 50 percent over two years, and our average return on this fund is 25 percent! I don't know about you, but that is criminal in my book. Is that numerical average a technically correct number? Yes. But did you experience a 25 percent rate of return? Nope. There is a big difference between *investor* results and *investment* results. There is a big difference between *average* returns and *actual* returns.

## Average vs. Actual Returns

So, we meet with a broker who says that was a "paper loss" and "don't worry about it." I had someone actually say to me, "I've heard the statistics that the stock market's averaged 10 percent over the past 30 years." They were using that statistic as a justification for leaving 100 percent of their assets in the market as they approached retirement. I have to say something about this.

First of all, the stock market average is about 7 ¾ percent. The 10 percent figure may have been closer to the truth a couple of decades ago, but this last decade (2000-2010) has flattened out the curve considerably. Market watchers call it the "lost decade." Why? Because when you put all the ups and downs on the board and then flatten them out, you went nowhere.

Secondly, averages are fine, but it's the timing I am interested in if I am near retirement age. A loss is not a "paper loss" if I have to take money out of the stock market to live on. If you are on the wrong end of something called the "sequence of returns," you will experience the phenomenon first hand. Consider the following hypothetical example.

## The Sequence of Returns Trap

In our hypothetical example, Jerry and Tom are two typical retirees. They are both age 65. Financially speaking, they are identical twins. They both start out with retirement savings totaling $500,000 and, when they hit 65, decide to retire. Oh yeah... all their money is in the stock market.

They each begin withdrawing 5 percent annually from their accounts because that's the amount their broker told them they should be able to take out and not deplete the account. Made sense to them. Why not? After all, the market *averaged* much more than that, didn't it? They figured $25,000 per year, plus their Social Security income, ought to carry them through a comfortable retirement for the rest of their lives.

| Jerry's Market Losses: | Tom's Market Losses: |
|---|---|
| -10.14% at age 65<br>-13.04% at age 66<br>-23.37% at age 67 | -23.37% at age 87<br>-13.04% at age 88<br>-10.14% at age 89 |

| Jerry | | | | Tom | | | |
|---|---|---|---|---|---|---|---|
| Age | Hypothetical stock market gains or losses | Withdrawal at start of year | Nest egg at start of year | Age | Hypothetical stock market gains or losses | Withdrawal at start of year | Nest egg at start of year |
| **64** | | | **$500,000** | **64** | | | **$500,000** |
| 65 | -10.14% | $25,000 | $500,000 | 65 | 12.78% | $25,000 | $500,000 |
| 66 | -13.04% | $25,750 | $426,839 | 66 | 23.45% | $25,750 | $535,716 |
| 67 | -23.37% | $26,523 | $348,776 | 67 | 26.38% | $26,523 | $629,575 |
| 68 | 14.62% | $27,318 | $246,956 | 68 | 3.53% | $27,318 | $762,140 |
| 69 | 2.03% | $28,138 | $251,750 | 69 | 13.62% | $28,138 | $760,755 |
| 70 | 12.40% | $28,982 | $228,146 | 70 | 3.00% | $28,982 | $832,396 |
| 71 | 27.25% | $29,851 | $223,862 | 71 | -38.49% | $29,851 | $827,524 |
| 72 | -6.65% | $30,747 | $246,879 | 72 | 26.38% | $30,747 | $490,684 |
| 73 | 26.31% | $31,669 | $201,956 | 73 | 19.53% | $31,669 | $581,270 |
| 74 | 4.46% | $32,619 | $215,084 | 74 | 26.67% | $32,619 | $656,916 |
| 75 | 7.06% | $33,598 | $190,610 | 75 | 31.10% | $33,598 | $790,788 |
| 76 | -1.54% | $34,606 | $168,090 | 76 | 20.26% | $34,606 | $991,981 |
| 77 | 34.11% | $35,644 | $131,429 | 77 | 34.11% | $35,644 | $1,151,375 |
| 78 | 20.26% | $36,713 | $128,458 | 78 | -1.54% | $36,713 | $1,496,314 |
| 79 | 31.01% | $37,815 | $110,335 | 79 | 7.06% | $37,815 | $1,437,133 |
| 80 | 26.67% | $38,949 | $95,008 | 80 | 4.46% | $38,949 | $1,498,042 |
| 81 | 19.53% | $40,118 | $71,009 | 81 | 26.31% | $40,118 | $1,524,231 |
| 82 | 26.38% | $36,923 | $36,923 | 82 | -6.56% | $41,321 | $1,874,535 |
| 83 | -38.49% | $0 | $0 | 83 | 27.25% | $42,561 | $1,712,970 |
| 84 | 3.00% | | | 84 | 12.40% | $43,838 | $2,125,604 |
| 85 | 13.62% | | | 85 | 2.03% | $45,153 | $2,339,923 |
| 86 | 3.53% | | | 86 | 14.37% | $46,507 | $2,341,297 |
| 87 | 26.38% | | | 87 | -23.27% | $47,903 | $2,630,297 |
| 88 | 23.45% | | | 88 | -13.04% | $49,340 | $1,978,993 |
| 89 | 12.78% | | | 89 | -10.14% | $50,820 | $1,677,975 |
| | **Average Return** | **Total Withdrawal** | | | **Average Return** | **Total Withdrawal** | |
| | 8.03% | $500,000 | | | 8.03% | $911,482 | |

They anticipated inflation, so they planned to bump up the withdrawal by 3 percent per year. So it would be $25,000 the first year, $27,750 the second year, $26,552.50 the third year and so on. For the purposes of this illustration, Jerry and Tom's assets are all invested in an index fund that tracks the movement of the market like a shadow. Whatever the market does, their account does. Let's be generous and say that they both experience an *average gain* of 8.03 percent over a 24-year period. What we did here used an actual slice of market history, so this is realistic.

Jerry and Tom are financially identical twins except for one big fact: *they were born years apart.* Jerry is much younger than Tom. What transpires in Jerry's account at age 65 happens in Tom's account at age 89. Do you see where we are going here? We want to show you the effect *timing* has on your *actual* returns and what a difference the sequence of returns makes in a retirement account. Jerry and Tom each had years of gains and years of losses. They both experience one three-year period of consecutive losses. While the losses were identical, they hit Jerry early in retirement and hit Tom toward the end.

Can you see what a difference the timing of the returns makes when you are retiring? Jerry ended up running out of money at age 83 because he was making steady withdrawals. His account was losing on the front end and the back end. The effect on Jerry's account was much worse than it was on Tom's.

So when brokers tout *average returns* and talk about *paper losses,* reach back and make sure your wallet is in your pocket. When they tell you to just look at the statistics, and how the market has averaged 10 percent per year (or 7 percent per year, for that matter), be careful. The inference is that your nest egg will grow at the same rate. It *could,* but it probably won't. How it affects your retirement all depends on the sequence of your returns.

## The Perfect Investment?

Sometimes when I conduct pro bono retirement planning workshops, I like to have a little fun with the audience by taking a little trip to Wall Street. If we could go to Wall Street and have them design for us the perfect financial instrument for retirement — one that would do anything we want it to do — what would we order? I go to the whiteboard and list their responses as we have the conversation.

One of the first things I hear is *guarantee of principle.* That is only natural. We do not want to lose anything we have gained, especially not about when we are ready to quit working. So I jot that one down. Then someone will say "good growth," or "high dividends." Either way, that translates to *good returns.* Could we say between 5 percent and 10 percent, given today's investment climate, would be a good rate of return? Yes, they reply. What next?

"No fees," someone will say. They probably have in mind the high hidden fees of mutual funds and variable annuities.

"Liquidity," another calls out.

I get that. You want to have access to your money if you need to. And you want high returns with no losses. Wouldn't we all like a repeat of the 1990s when we could expect a 25 percent return and no losses?

"Probate-proof," someone says. In other words, you want to be able to pass the amount of money you have saved on to your loved ones when you die. You don't want it eroded by lawyers and lawsuits. I get that.

So, the fundamental desire of the crowd seems to be a product that would go up when the market goes up but would be immune from downturns, would be completely safe, would have good, steady returns, would be probate-proof and would be liquid.

## The Truth About Annuities

Is it just me, or does it seem that every time we plug in the word "annuity" into an Internet search engine, we get a sandstorm of conflicting opinions and misinformation? What is it about this financial instrument — the annuity — that polarizes people? Some folks swear at them, and others swear by them. Why is that?

Part of the bias comes from a misunderstanding of what the word "annuity" means. When you say the word, "automobile," for instance, you could be talking about anything from a pickup truck to a race car. It's the same way with annuities. As we talked about in Chapter One, there are many types of annuities out there: traditional fixed annuities, immediate annuities, variable annuities and fixed index annuities. There is a world of difference in these annuities and how they function. The one thing they all have in common is that they are all issued by insurance companies.

### Variable Annuities

I have found that most of the time, when people react negatively to the word "annuity," they are thinking of *variable* annuities. Variable annuities bear little resemblance to fixed annuities and fixed index annuities. Variable annuities are market investments packaged in an annuity wrapper primarily. Why? Mainly for the tax deferment. Can you lose money in a variable annuity? Yes, whereas with fixed annuities and fixed index annuities, your principal is guaranteed by the insurance company issuing the product. That is why I often don't recommend variable annuities for older investors who are approaching retirement age. They may appeal to younger investors who want a tax-deferred market investment with what amounts to a life insurance policy tacked on. But for those who are risk-averse, it may not be a good idea. Variable annuities usually come with more fees than their fixed annuity distant cousins.

I am not the only one who advocates caution when it comes to variable annuities. I recently saw a headline in Forbes magazine: "9 Reasons You Need to Avoid Variable Annuities." AARP, the mouthpiece for millions of retired Americans, published the following headline: "Variable annuities are not for those already retired or near retirement."

The problem is the media often throws the baby out with the bathwater. When they discuss the negatives of variable annuities, they fail to specify that not all annuities are alike. Could it be that many reporters don't know the difference? I think so.

## Skin in the Game

If I were to say to you, "You should be buying Wal-Mart stock," You would probably say to me, "If it's such a good deal, then how much stock are you buying?" And it would be a fair question. So what about annuities? Do I have any "skin in the game" as they say? Yes, as a matter of fact, I do! As this is written, I have about $1 million in fixed index annuities. When I rolled my 401(k) over into an IRA, I placed those assets into an FIA. I also have my wife's IRA invested in a fixed index annuity. As we approach retirement age, we are very cautious about investment risk. I don't know about you, but at age 65, I don't like seeing those little parentheses on my financial statements.

The reason I am telling you this is not to impress you, but to impress upon you that I do not recommend something I do not own myself. Fixed index annuities are growing so rapidly that they are scaring the dickens out of Wall Street. Don't get me wrong. If you are 25, you can afford to invest in the market and ride its unpredictable undulations. But if you are age 55, 60 or 65, you probably feel this way regarding your finances:

1. I don't want to outlive my money.

2. **I don't want another 9/11 happen and see my life savings evaporate overnight.**
3. **I want to be able to get to my money if I need it.**
4. **If I don't use it all, I want to be able to pass it along to my family in a tax-efficient manner.**

[5]

# Predator #5 — Banks

**LET ME START OUT** by saying I have nothing against banks. I love banks. I really do! They have this nice little arrangement called a "checking account" that eliminates the necessity of carrying large sums of cash around with you. They let you stroke a check or use a debit card when you want to buy something. It is very convenient! Most everyone I know of has one of these accounts. Most everyone I know of has a bank credit card, too. Behind every credit card is a bank, and you know what a necessity for traveling credit cards have become these days.

So why do I list banks among financial predators? First of all, I'm not talking about the smiling, pleasant folks behind the counter at your local neighborhood bank. I'm talking about the false sense of security projected by the banking industry—the illusory impression that banks are bastions of safety and the epitome of trustworthiness. Such notions are simply not true and have caused personal disaster. It was the shady misdeeds of big banks that nearly capsized the national economy in 2008. The attitude of the big boys on Wall Street trickles down and permeates the entire U.S. banking system.

## "Please, Trust Me!"

When I hear someone preface what they are about to say with the words, "Trust me..." it always makes me doubt what comes next. It suggests that what they said up to that point may have been less than trustworthy. If not, then why do they now find it necessary to ask for our trust, right? Have you ever noticed that banks go out of their way to establish trust? Take bank names, for example. You never hear of names like "Lester and Ethel's Bank" or "Accounts-R-Us." For some reason, banks need to have names with a serious, imposing tone like "First National Bank and Trust." A lot of bank names incorporate the word "trust." And they like to be "first." I suppose it's an American thing. We like to be first, and if we are going to put our money somewhere, we want to be able to trust those people. That explains the ornate buildings and the stuffy names.

One of the most puzzling names for a bank is Fifth Third Bank, headquartered in Cincinnati, Ohio. No, I'm not making this up! Sounds like a fourth-grade lesson in fractions gone awry, but it is an actual bank name. When I first heard it, I thought it was a joke. What? Did four other banks named "Third Bank" fail, and now we have the fifth in a series? If we had one in my neighborhood, I would probably have my checking account there just because I like the peculiar name.

But I am straying from the subject.

My profession requires that I pay attention to what is happening on Wall Street and strive to understand what goes on behind the headlines. I don't think I have ever heard the expression "too big to fail" as much as I did in the year 2008. When banks fail, it is one thing. But when banks that are "too big to fail" start to topple, it lets you know that something is systemically wrong. The scary stuff that happened with the big banks in 2008 was an eye-opener for many—or at least it should have been.

## Housing Bubble Trouble

In 2002, the wheels of the economy started to turn again as the nation began to recover from the dot-com recession. The folks on Wall Street were whistling "Happy Days Are Here Again" and the construction industry started waking up. In 2004 and 2005, the housing boom was in full bloom. New home communities were springing up across the nation like dandelions after a summer rain. Contractors were hiring anyone who could swing a hammer. Every business along the supply chain was making money, from the lumber salesman to the land speculator. Banks were happy. Money was flowing like water and mortgages were easy to come by. If you had a pulse, you could get a loan. The way the banks figured it, the value of property was going to continue to go up. It didn't matter to them if buyers defaulted on loans. They could just repossess the property that served as collateral for the loan and recycle it for even more profit than before.

Home buyers were in a feeding frenzy. They wanted to get that down payment on the books as quickly as possible before the price went up. Real estate was touted as the greatest investment ever! How could you go wrong?

Fanning the flames of the boom were low-interest rates and extremely creative loan packages. "Piggyback" loans were in vogue. That's when you don't have enough money for the down payment, so you get not one, but two mortgages on the home—the first mortgage for the down payment and the second mortgage for the rest of the loan.

When the housing boom was in full swing, the banks were practically giving away home loans under the banner of what they called "creative lending." No job? No problem. Have no idea how you are going to ever pay the mortgage back? No problem. The banks came up with something called a No-Doc-NINA. That's a no-document, no-income, no-asset loan. It essentially meant the value of the property would stand good for the loan. Exotic adjustable-rate mortgages were all the rage in those days. They remind me of those credit card offers — no interest for six months to get you hooked and then 18-20 percent interest. ARM mortgages lured you in with a very low interest rate to start and the possibility of a stiff increase in the interest rate three years later. One of the most exotic mortgages the banks came up with in those days was the "interest-only" loan. Just like it sounds, you never pay on the principal — just the interest. The banks wanted to get the payments as low as possible so they could move the merchandise. According to some reports, average home prices more than doubled in America from 1997 to 2006. Banks were behaving as though the party would never end.

Do you see a problem with any of this? It was a train-wreck waiting to happen, and it would only be a few years before it did. The chickens began circling the henhouse in 2006 and they came home to roost in 2007. With home prices dropping like a stone, it was soon apparent the housing boom was over and by the fall of 2008, defaulting on home loans was epidemic. Foreclosure signs began springing up in front lawns all across the country and all of this spelled doom for the banks who had spawned the mess.

## Who Was Watching the Watchers?

The role of the banking system in the economy is that of an intermediary. Those who have money in excess deposit it in a bank, and the bank lends money to those who need it. From a high-altitude view, it's just that simple. But there have to be rules to keep the banking industry honest. Unethical practices by banks can ruin a healthy economy.

The role of the Federal Reserve System is to regulate and supervise the banks. The Fed is supposed to make sure that banks are sound and safe. Ultimately, the Fed works for the people, not the banks. They are expected to keep an eye on the banks and make sure the rights of bank customers are not violated. There is no nice way to put it. The Fed was asleep at the wheel in 2006 when the seeds of the financial crisis were sown. The buck doesn't stop there. The Fed works under the supervision of Congress. In short, no one was watching the watchers.

In 2006, the big investment banks on Wall Street were doing a brisk business. Merrill Lynch, Goldman Sachs, Bear Stearns, Lehman Brothers, Morgan Stanley — the "too-big-to-fail" gang — were all leveraged to the hilt and on shaky ground, financially. And they were wading deeper and deeper into the quicksand. Their financial underpinnings were all those bad loans made with easy money in the days of the housing boom.

The smallest of the "too big" banks was Bear Stearns. It was the first to go. How could this be possible? Not "The Bear!" Bear Stearns' reputation was that of a reliable, conservative firm, one of the soundest banks on Wall Street. In March of 2008, it took only 72 hours for the truth to come out that "The Bear" was nearly insolvent and was sitting on a mountain of bad debt. Bear Stearns was the object of what the financial newspapers called a "fire sale" and its stock was purchased for pennies on the dollar by JPMorgan Chase.

By October 2008, several other big banks were on the rocks. Some failed outright and others were targets of acquisition. Still others had to be bailed out by taxpayer dollars or became subject to government takeover. It was a mess. I remember during that time virtually every newscast started out with a report of the government having to rescue another bank. The list included the two mortgage giants, Fannie Mae (Federal National Mortgage Association) and Freddie Mac (Federal Home Loan Mortgage Corporation), as well as Lehman Brothers, Merrill Lynch, Washington Mutual, Wachovia and Citigroup.

The financial crisis of 2008 reminds me of the tsunami that hit Japan in March 2011. The earthquake and the giant ocean wave that struck that country lasted only a few hours but left enormous damage from which it would take years to recover. The banking collapse of 2008 was the worst economic disaster since the Great Depression. The Wall Street earthquake sent ripples of economic turmoil all around the world. Consider also the psychological damage these banks caused. How long will it be before we again trust these giant financial institutions as just and capable intermediaries of our commercial system?

## Derivatives

When rumors began to circulate in 2007 about the trouble the "too big" banks were in, we learned a new word — derivatives. When news reporters had to communicate to the general public why their tax dollars had to rescue big banks, they had to explain all about "derivatives" — certainly no household word. But if we didn't know what they were before, we quickly became educated.

In plain speech, a derivative is something based on something else. Peanut butter is a derivative of peanuts. In bank language, derivatives are financial instruments that assume their value from an underlying asset, such as an interest rate or an index. Here is where it gets hazy. It is *perceived* value. Derivatives have no value in and of themselves. They are valuable only to the extent of the value that others place on them. Sounds dangerous already, doesn't it? You can probably see where this is going.

The collateral for the mountain of debt these banks were accumulating turns out to be, when all is said and done, a house sitting on shifting sand. We are talking about billions and billions of dollars in loans the big banks made to wholesale banks, and the wholesale banks made to mortgage lenders, who in turn loaned money to the end users — and it was all backed up by nothing of substance. The ever-rising value of property was a self-inflating balloon kept aloft by banks making bad loans. The banks were flying on a wing and a prayer with no exit strategy.

There were warning signs that should have prevented the crisis, but greed blinded the bankers, and the Fed was like those three monkeys who cover their ears, eyes and mouth and proclaim they hear no evil, see no evil and speak no evil.

In the 2002 Berkshire Hathaway annual report, Warren Buffett said about derivatives:

> *"I view derivatives as time bombs, both for the parties that deal in them and the economic system. Basically these instruments call for money to change hands at some future date, with the amount to be determined by one or more reference items, such as interest rates, stock prices or currency values. Central banks and governments have so far found no effective way to control, or even monitor, the risks posed by these contracts... In my view, derivatives are financial weapons of mass destruction, carrying dangers that, while now latent, are potentially lethal."*

Wow! How prophetic! When Congress voted to bail out the mega banks, Uncle Sam became a partner in the mess, accepting the subprime mortgages, which were the root of the problem, as collateral. In September 2008, when Lehman Brothers declared bankruptcy, it was followed by the news that American International Group (AIG) was running out of cash attempting to cover the credit default swaps it had issued against mortgage-backed securities.

**The Dow Jones Industrial Average (DJIA) slipped hundreds of points per day. I remember watching the ticker on the financial channel on Sept. 29, 2008 — the day the Dow set a record for the biggest drop in history, losing 777 points in one day. They didn't have a name for it then, but the Great Recession, as it was later called, had started and the general population of the nation would have to reap the misery of what the big banks had sown.**

## Healing the Wounds

**As a financial advisor, I am on the front lines when economic disasters strike. I see it up close and personal. I saw what the banking crisis of 2008 did to people's lives. Those who were approaching retirement were hurt the worst, especially those who had entrusted Wall Street with their entire life's savings. On Oct. 8, 2008, before the crisis had even peaked, the Washington Post ran the headline, "Retirement Savings Lose $2 Trillion in 15 Months." On March 13, 2009, after the crisis had peaked and the smoke was beginning to clear, U.S. News and World Report ran the headline, "Retirement Accounts Have Now Lost $3.4 Trillion."**

**When we have our pro bono educational workshops, I hear some of the horror stories. In the fall of 2008, when the news about the big bank bailouts was in all the newspapers, I could see grave concern on the faces of those who attended a workshop on estate planning and tax review. People were worried. Many of them had worked hard all their lives to accumulate what was in their retirement funds and were seeing it blown away like loose dust in a stiff wind.**

**I could tell these people wanted answers, so I just set aside my prepared remarks and threw it open to questions and answers. It had just been on the news that the Dow had dropped nearly 1,000 points in two days, and that mega bank Lehman Brothers had declared bankruptcy.**

"Why didn't our broker warn us this could happen?" one gentleman asked.

There was no good answer. They didn't want to know about derivatives or credit default swaps. All they knew was their trust was shaken in institutions they had trusted and they had been personally injured by the betrayal.

"What should we do now?" asked one woman. "Our broker is saying 'hold on' but he doesn't understand that we were counting on that money for our retirement."

In some cases, individuals who were set to retire in their mid-60s would be forced to continue working until age 70 to make up for what they had lost. Others had to pare down their lifestyles dramatically. Some were forced to sell comfortable homes in a buyer's market — homes in which they had planned to live the rest of their lives — in an effort to make up for their portfolio losses.

I later met with many of these individuals in private sessions to salvage what remained of their wrecked financial lives and put them on a course where such hardship would not be repeated. I felt like a first responder doing triage after a natural disaster, trying to patch up financial wounds. When brokers told these people the markets would eventually recover, they weren't lying to them. Markets do recover. But the key word here is EVENTUALLY. In most cases, these folks didn't have time to wait on "eventually."

"Last year we had a little over $750,000 in our nest egg," lamented one couple. Their broker had advised them to place the money in a mixture of bonds, stocks, mutual funds and variable annuities. "That way, you're diversified," he had told them. The husband showed me their latest statement where he had circled the latest balance — a little more than $450,000.

"When I was in my 30s, that would have been a lot of money," said the husband. The couple owned and ran a small business that they had planned to sell. The way they figured it, with the proceeds of the sale of the business, combined with their Social Security, they could live comfortably, do some traveling and perhaps leave some money to their children when they passed away. Those plans were out the window now. It wasn't quite back to square one for these folks, but they would have to rebuild, and there was no way they could retire any time soon.

## Trust in Tatters

In February 2013, an article entitled "What's Inside America's Banks?" appeared in The Atlantic Monthly. The article said public trust in big banks was "as low as ever" four years after the financial crisis. The article went on to explain, "Sophisticated investors describe big banks as 'black boxes' that may still be concealing enormous risks — the sort that could again take down the economy." The Great Recession spawned by the big banks cost Americans an estimated $16 trillion. Even if that money is eventually recovered, the fabric of the people's trust has been irreparably damaged.

The effects of natural disasters don't last forever. Look at Mount St. Helens in Washington. The volcano made a moonscape out of millions of acres, but here and there green trees are poking out of the silt and ash, and wildlife is returning. However, the mountain blew up in 1980, and it will never quite be the same. The greatest damage caused by the banking crisis and the financial meltdown of 2008 was the erosion of trust. Could such a thing happen again? We would be foolish not to think so. In the words of philosopher George Santayana, "Those who cannot learn from history are doomed to repeat it."

## How Safe Are Banks?

In 1933, the nation was in the grip of the Great Depression. Homeless people slept in makeshift huts in public parks and lined up for free hot meals at soup kitchens in major cities. The jobless rate was 25 percent; 11 million people were unemployed. More than 4,000 banks failed in 1933 alone.

President Franklin Roosevelt gave a speech to the nation and explained what today you may think is an obvious truth, but apparently many at the time didn't know. Here is an excerpt from a March 12, 1933, speech regarding the banking crisis:

> *"First of all let me state the simple fact that when you deposit money in a bank the bank does not put the money into a safe deposit vault. It invests your money in many different forms of credit-bonds, commercial paper, mortgages and many other kinds of loans. In other words, the bank puts your money to work to keep the wheels of industry and of agriculture turning around. A comparatively small part of the money you put into the bank is kept in currency — an amount which in normal times is wholly sufficient to cover the cash needs of the average citizen. In other words the total amount of all the currency in the country is only a small fraction of the total deposits in all of the banks."*

On June 16, 1933, Roosevelt signed into law the Banking Act of 1933, which established the Federal Deposit Insurance Corporation (FDIC). Its stated purpose was to reinstall trust in banks by ensuring that, even if a bank were to fail, the depositor would not lose money. As this book is written, if you have money in a savings or checking account at a bank that meets the criteria set by the FDIC (and most all of them do), then your money is insured up to $250,000 per depositor. The insurance also applies to CDs, bank IRAs and money market deposit accounts.

I remember seeing a photograph online back in March 2008 of a line of depositors that stretched down a city block and out of sight in front of IndyMac Bank, headquartered in Pasadena, California. It had hit the news that the bank was in trouble, and the people were there to withdraw their money. In those days, accounts were only insured up to $100,000, and some of those poor people learned that the hard way. The bank was subsequently taken over by the U.S. Treasury Department and its doors were closed.

IndyMac, with its $95 billion, was small potatoes compared to the September 2008 fall of Washington Mutual Bank. The WaMu failure was the largest in history, with a reported $300 billion in assets at the time of its collapse.

The bottom line? Banks can and do fail. According to data collected from the FDIC, as of this writing, 482 banks have failed since 2009, costing the FDIC's Deposit Insurance Fund more than $472 billion.

## Banks vs. Insurance Companies

Historically, banks have failed while insurance companies have survived. Why is that? The government heavily regulates both of these economic institutions. The Center for Insurance Policy and Research released a study in 2013 entitled, "Study on the State of the Life Insurance Industry." The study observed that during the 10 years of economic turmoil between 2002 and 2012, the life insurance industry "significantly outperformed the banking industry." If both the banks and the insurance industry are subject to strict regulation, why would one outperform the other?

The answer lies in the stricter standard applied to insurance companies. The law requires insurance companies to maintain reserves equal to 100 percent of their liabilities, whereas banks are required to maintain only around 5 percent reserves to back up their deposits. Insurance companies are regulated at the state level and are closely monitored to make sure they keep adequate reserves, whereas banks are governed at a national level by the Federal Reserve and the United States Treasury Department. If an insurance company starts to fail, the state requires a stable insurance company take it over. Thanks to a system known as "statutory accounting," insurance companies are forced to keep a dollar on hand for every dollar they have obligated. This system keeps people who have invested in insurance products from losing money due to company failure. Investors in fixed annuities and fixed index annuities, for example, are protected by several layers of guarantees. The first level is the dollar-for-dollar reserve maintained by insurance companies. The second level is the state guaranty funds maintained in each state as required by state law. The state requires that a financially sound insurance company assume the books of one in default so that the policy holder is never left in the lurch. The third level of protection is re-insurance — something that all insurance companies do to spread the risk.

Maybe that's why, in the 1930s, the insurance industry posted gains while banks were failing. With all that on the table, you can see why I have to bite my tongue and force myself from rolling my eyes when someone asks about an insurance product, "Hey wait... is that FDIC insured?" as if being insured by the FDIC is as rock-solid a guarantee of safety one can possibly imagine. Can the FDIC go broke? As early as 2009 I started seeing headlines suggesting that when all the "too-big-to-fail" megabanks were toppling, the FDIC itself was in danger of failing.

What many fail to understand is the "C" in FDIC stands for "corporation." That's right, the FDIC is a corporation just like any other commercial operation that is incorporated and yes, it can go bankrupt. Of course, as long as the government can print money, the FDIC can borrow it — up to $500 billion as I write this. What's a few more billion when the national debt at the time of this writing exceeds $18 trillion?

When someone asks, "Dave, is this insurance-based strategy FDIC insured?" I tell them that I certainly hope it's not FDIC insured. Why do I say that? Because if the FDIC has 37 cents for every $100 that I stick in the bank, I feel a little shaky about that. But if I put $100 with an insurance company, by law they must maintain at least $100, and in some cases as much as $105, in reserve. It's not a voluntary option — the law requires it!

Let me reiterate that I am not anti-bank. Do I have money in the bank? Yes. Do I think that banks are going under? No. I just like going into things with my eyes wide open and I recommend that for all my clients.

Recently, I called the FDIC, and I asked them a question: "If my bank goes under, how long do you take to get me my money? I want to know what the law says of how long it will take to get me my money." The lady replied, "What we have done in the past is..." I interrupted her, "I don't mean to be disagreeable, ma'am, But I really don't care what you have done in the past, what you usually do or what you like to do. I want to know what the 'big book' says."

"Would you like to talk to my supervisor?" she said.

"Yes, thank you. I would." I said.

When the supervisor gets on the phone, he too began speaking in terms of what *usually* takes place and what they *typically* do. Again, I politely but firmly asked him what the law says about how long it would take me as a depositor to receive my cash if a bank failed.

Would it surprise you to know that there is no hard, fast rule? Would it surprise you to know that the FDIC is only required to pay me "as soon as possible?" Don't believe me? Here's the exact wording taken from the voluminous Federal Deposit Insurance Act:

> ***"Payment of the insured deposits is required by statute to be made 'as soon as possible' (per 12 U.S.C. § 1821(f))."***

**Could it take up to 99 years as some critics of the FDIC claim? Impossible to answer such a question since there is no definitive time-limit, isn't it? I don't think anyone is ever going to have a situation where the bank goes under, and they have to wait 99 years for their claim to be paid. But without specific rules, it's a moot point.**[11]

## The Story of Ralph and Gladys

**Before we move along to other predators, I must tell you the story of Ralph and Gladys. Ralph is a pretty conservative guy. He and Gladys are out for a ride. Ralph is driving, and he stops at a gas station to fill up the tank.**

**"Honey, I'm going to have to go inside and pay," he says. "This pump doesn't take credit cards."**

**While he is inside, he does something he has never done. He impulsively buys one of those scratch-off lottery tickets. This time, to his utter delight and amazement, he wins $1,000! He rushes back to the car and tells Gladys. She makes him show her the cash before she believes him and then she, too, squeals with delight.**

**When the excitement dies down, they both start discussing what they are going to do with the money. As they are driving down the highway, they pass a bank, and they both have the same idea at once. So they pull into the bank with intentions of depositing the money for safekeeping. It is a beautiful bank, with marble columns outside and rich thick carpet inside. They enter, clutching the wad of bills,**

---

[11] **Federal Deposit Insurance Corporation. April 20, 2014. FDIC Law, Regulations, Related Acts, "1000 – Federal Deposit Insurance Act." https://www.fdic.gov/regulations/laws/rules/1000-1240.html.**

and are greeted by a pleasant man who asks them their names. He invites them to follow him to a nicely appointed office. Their fatal mistake was to walk on the carpet in the first place... but more about that in a moment. They tell him the story and explain to him that they don't quite know what they should do with the money. He tells them that they should put it into something called a CD. You and I know what a CD is, right? Certificate of disappointment? The man tells Ralph and Gladys if they put their $1,000 in a CD the bank will pay them 5 percent interest (this is an *old* story). That means that a year from now they will receive a whopping $50 on their $1,000.

Ralph and Gladys look at each other and nod to each other that it sounds like a good deal. A year later they go to the bank and, sure enough, their account has grown by $50.

"Let's not compound the interest," says Ralph. "Let's spend the $50 tonight on dinner at Superior Steakhouse."

So as they are getting ready to go blow the $50 on an evening out, they hear a knock on the door. When they open the door, there stands a well-dressed gentleman who tells Ralph that he is with the Internal Revenue Service. He says he noticed the couple had just received $50 from the bank, and Ralph explains to him about the CD.

"Well, you know you are going to have to pay taxes on that," says the IRS man, clearing his throat and extending his hand. "The way I figure it, you owe Uncle Sam $15, and since I am in the neighborhood, I'll just go ahead and collect that money now."

Ralph forks over the $15 and starts to finish getting ready for dinner when there is another knock on the door.

"Who in the world could that be?" asks Gladys. Ralph goes to the door and opens it. Another man, dressed much like the last man is standing there.

"Did you just pay a man $15?" he asks. Ralph acknowledges that he did.

"Well, that was the Feds," he said. "I'm with the state, and we want $5." Irritated, Ralph digs into his pocket and pays the man $5 and the man walks away. Once again, he goes to finish getting ready for dinner when he hears yet another knock at the door.

"Who could it be this time?" grumbles Ralph as he opens the door.

"Hi! I'm with the Social Security Administration," says the third man. "It has come to our attention that you earned $50 interest on your $1,000 CD at the bank. That generated a 1099 on your tax return. That amount is just enough to put you over the Social Security threshold, so you have to pay an additional $4 withholding."

Poor Ralph explains to Gladys that the $50 they were going to use to pay for a nice steak dinner with all the trimmings at Superior Steakhouse has dwindled down to $26, and they will have to go for the special at Applebee's instead.

Isn't that the way of things? No, I am not anti-bank, but I don't know a nice way to put it that investing money in banks may not be the best thing to help you reach your financial goals. You get very little return on your investment and what you do get is fully taxable. If you are retired and receiving Social Security, and you are concerned with safety of principal and you don't trust the stock market, there are several alternatives that a competent financial advisor can explain to you.

[6]

# Predator #6 — Family and Friends

**I KNOW WHAT YOU'RE THINKING.** Family and friends? Predators? No way! And before you toss this book in the nearest trash bin for even suggesting the idea, please let me explain that I love my family, and I love my friends and you should too.

Sometimes when I give talks at public educational events, my son, Colin, introduces me as his "best friend." Well, the feeling is mutual. I was the best man at his wedding, an honor that I still cherish. We work together and play together. He even calls me "Dave" instead of Dad, something with which I am entirely comfortable.

The other day, we were talking about mortgages.

"I want to get a mortgage, Dave. What do you think of a 30-year, adjustable rate mortgage — one you pay every two weeks?"

There are two reasons why it is altogether appropriate for him to ask me such a question, and entirely fitting that I should answer: First, I am his father, and as such will give him advice that is in his best interests with no ulterior motive, such as profit, in mind. Second, I know what I'm talking about. I have studied mortgages from one end to the other, and I can answer the question from a point of experience and knowledge. If he asks his next door neighbor, who may drive a truck for a living and play golf on the weekends (not that there is anything wrong with either of those things), he may get advice that is well-meant, but misguided and off the mark. His neighbor will almost certainly not know as much as I do on the subject.

So that's my point. Family and friends will give you financial advice, and they will mean well, but if the advice is off the mark, it can cost you thousands — even hundreds of thousands — of dollars.

## Wrong Directions From Good People

I grew up in New Jersey, but I have lived in Louisiana long enough to qualify as an honorary native of the state, and I can honestly say my heart is here. It's not the beautiful bayous and the mild weather that I love so much (and the food, don't forget the food), but the people. I have never met a greater bunch of folks than those who live and work in this part of the world. Warm, friendly and generous. If you ask them for help, they will bend over backward to give it to you and ask for nothing in return. It's just how Louisianans roll.

The only downside to this spirit, I have noticed, is when it comes to giving directions. If you are driving through rural Louisiana and you stop at a gas station to get directions, you will seldom hear, "I don't know, pal," like you would in New Jersey. You will get the very best reckoning they can muster, even if they haven't a clue. And they won't call you "pal." Maybe "partner," the closer you get to the Texas border, but not "pal." This trait of wanting to help you, even if they don't know the information you are seeking, is as charming as it is confounding sometimes. Even if their directions are way off target, there is one thing that cannot be questioned — their good intentions and desire to help.

**It's like that with family members, too. They love you and want the best for you, and they aren't at all shy about offering their opinion when it comes to financial decisions. And why is it most people tend to rely on the advice they receive from Mom, Dad, good old Uncle Allen or their cousin, than that of a fully trained professional? Easy! They trust their family, and they assume right off the bat that the professional is motivated by profit. Score it this way:**

- **Accurate advice provided with detailed proof and statistics — 10 points.**
- **Relationship with someone they feel they can trust — 90 points.**
- **The problem comes in when the trusted advice is the wrong advice.**

## Money Attracts Advice

**To what extent are friends and family willing to give you financial advice? Say you won the lottery. You will be amazed at how many friends and family members you suddenly have around you. I did some research on the subject and discovered most people who win a large sum of money in a lottery do not have it long. In fact, from what I read, regardless of how large the sum, there's an 80 percent chance you will blow through it within two years.**[12]

**Remember the Publisher's Clearinghouse Sweepstakes and how we all daydreamed about Ed McMahon showing up at our door holding up a check for $1 million? I remember a study where researchers went back 20 years and surveyed the people who actually won the sweepstakes. Eighteen out of 20 had gone through the mil-**

---

[12] **GoldenGirlFinance.com. Yahoo! Finance. April 24, 2013. "Riches to rags: Why most lottery winners end up broke." https://ca.finance.yahoo.com/news/riches-rags-why-most-lottery-winners-end-broke-180227163.html.**

lion dollars in two years. In some cases, the winners squandered the money on extravagances. But in the majority of instances, they listened to the advice of friends and family on how to invest the money and multiply their fortune. I am sure, however, that if you had wanted to start a fight with one of them at the time they were following the errant advice, all you would have had to do was suggest that perhaps, just maybe, their friends and family didn't know what they were talking about.

An example of this is the fact that only 4 percent of National Football League players who become millionaires stay millionaires. That means that 96 percent end up in the same economic shape as they were in before they signed their lucrative contracts. Why is that? It is typical for people, when they get a hefty lump sum of money, to assume that it will last forever. Typically, they go out and buy a Harley Davidson motorcycle or two, a luxury speed boat, a hot car and other expensive toys. At that rate, it doesn't take them long to burn through a million dollars.

I have a client who is around 60 years of age who has a 42-year-old daughter. Unfortunately, the daughter's husband was killed in an accident. The husband's life was insured, and she received a check for $250,000 from New York Life. They asked me to help them invest $100,000 of the money. I put the money in a safe investment for them that, after two years, grew to almost $113,000. Not bad, right? So what did they do with the rest of the money? Her family and friends advised her to pay off the mortgage on her house. Does that sound like good advice? In certain circumstances, it can be wise to pay off a mortgage and own your home free and clear, but in this case it turned out not to be a good idea.

The daughter had a 10/20/10 auto insurance policy. The first two numbers refer to the limits on bodily injury coverage. So she had coverage of up to $10,000 per individual injured in an accident and $20,000 for all persons who could be injured in an accident. The last number, 10, meant that she was covered for $10,000 in property damage. In other words, if she injured or killed someone in an automobile accident, the car insurance would pay only $10,000 for medical treatment to treat the person's injuries or $10,000 for their death. That was it.

As things turned out, tragedy visited the family again when the daughter was involved in another automobile accident in which she was ruled at fault, and the driver of the other car was seriously injured. I knew how these things usually worked. The attorneys representing the injured driver would likely file a lawsuit. If the liability insurance policy only paid $10,000, that was unlikely to satisfy them. Now what? Where would the lawyers likely look for damages? The daughter's estate. All of her assets, even her paid-for home. There were some long faces when it began to sink in that the woman she had hit was probably going to own her home. So much for the advice from family and friends.

About 18 months later I was able to discuss it with her. I asked her how much of the $150,000 she had left. She said there was nothing left. Her financial situation had changed when her husband died. She was still working, and she was receiving Social Security benefits. She was also receiving workers' compensation payments because he was killed in a work-related accident. She was earning more in the way of weekly income than ever before. She had borrowed money to put in a backyard pool. She had also been generous with her money and paid off her brother's school loan.

Years later, after she had recovered somewhat from her financial difficulties, we had a chat about setting up money for her children's education.

"I just want them to get so much per year," she said. "If they get it in a lump sum they might squander it."

When you get information from family and friends, you need to be sensitive to the source and always get a second opinion on the advice. Her family and friends had great intentions when they told her to pay off her house, but in her case, it wasn't the prudent thing to do.

## Parentheses in Her 401(k)

The following actually happened to me in 2002: A woman had a 401(k) that she said was doing quite well — making lots of money. Remember, this was in 2002. I had been following the stock market very closely, and I knew nobody was making money in their 401(k) plans that year and told her I thought she might be mistaken.

"No, it's true," she said. "All the people who work around me want to know what funds I'm in. I just tell them that I picked some good ones, and they are all making a lot of money."

I told her that I didn't want to be negative, but I had been closely following the stock market and I found it difficult to believe her 401(k) was going up when everyone else's was experiencing losses. I asked her if she would mind showing me her latest statement, and she was happy to do so.

"See," she said, pointing to the paper. "On December 31, I had $10,000; on March 31, I had $11,000."

I asked her if she was making regular contributions and she said she was — around $600 per month, not counting the employer matching portion.

"Do you know what these parentheses mean," I asked her. She said no.

When it dawned on her that she was losing money, not making money in her 401(k), she put her hands to her face and said, "Oh, no!"

The poor woman had no idea.

I told her not to be too distraught. She was relatively young, and I expressed to her that, thanks to dollar-cost averaging, if she continued making her regular contributions her 401(k) would probably recover in a few years.

"That's not what's bothering me," she said. "What about all those people who were following my advice?"

## Other 401(k) Mistakes People Make

While we are on the subject, according to the Investment Company Institute, more than 50 million Americans had around $4.4 trillion invested in 401(k)s as of June 30, 2014. From my conversations with many of these folks, I don't think most people know very much about their 401(k) accounts. All they seem to know is that a portion of their paycheck goes into this account whose name sounds peculiarly like a vitamin pill and, when they retire, it will give a measure of financial security.

When the subject of 401(k)s comes up in the educational seminars I sponsor, I try to point out some of the most common mistakes people make in these tax-deferred, employer-sponsored retirement plans — mistakes that can cost them thousands of dollars. Here are a few:

When people change jobs or retire, they have a choice to make. Do they leave their 401(k) as it is, in the hands of the custodian appointed by their former employer? Do they cash it out and put the money in their checking account until they can figure out what do to with it? Do they roll it over into another tax-deferred retirement savings account, such as a self-directed IRA? Do they ask for a check and spend all the money on toys and expensive vacations? All but one of those options could be a huge mistake.

### Cashing It Out

You would be amazed at how many people go for the cash-out option. Fidelity Investments, one of the largest custodians of 401(k)

**plans in the country, says that more than one-third of American workers cash out their retirement plans, often when they change jobs or retire. It's human nature at work. They see that big pile of money sitting there and it is tempting to convert it to cash. To be fair, perhaps some of them are in a financial crunch or have pressing credit card debt they wish to pay off. Regardless, it may be a mistake except in the direst of circumstances to cash out your 401(k). Here's why: Not only are you (a) penalized 10 percent if you are under 59 ½, but you are (b) taxed on the money you withdraw (federal, state and local taxes), and (c) you miss out on all the earnings the account may have generated.**

**It may be tempting to take the money and run, but you don't get the full amount. The IRS requires the employer to withhold 20 percent. If you take money from a qualified account and leave the money in your checking account for more than 60 days, it becomes ordinary income and is taxed accordingly.**

## Leaving Your 401(k) With Your Former Employer

**This option is usually imprudent to do so because you lose a measure of control. You probably won't keep track of the account like you should and, if there is a hefty sum in there, that's a lot of money to lose track of. An exception would be if you have a loan you are repaying to your plan. Moving the account could gum up those works. I can think of one word that constitutes another reason for moving the 401(k) from a former employer: Enron. Remember the Enron 401(k) scandal? At its zenith as a corporation, Enron stock was on a roll, and 62 percent of the 401(k) was invested in company stock. If you hitch your wagon to one star like that and it comes crashing down, there goes your retirement security with it.**

## Paying Too Much in Fees

I have noticed most people just don't want to bother themselves with the details of their investments; they just want results. As one fellow put it: "Don't tell me about the labor pains; just show me the baby." There are fees and charges associated with their 401(k) investments and, if you aren't paying attention, you could be paying too much. This could retard the growth of your retirement account. Most 401(k) plans are invested in mutual funds and these funds charge fees that are usually shown as net returns. In other words, they are subtracted from your gains or added to your losses *before* your annual return is calculated.

How do you know if you are paying too much in fees? One way is to ask. Most large employers have human resources people there to help you understand such things. Your 401(k) plan website is a treasure trove of information. Also, look at your statement. Fund expenses may be buried in the fine print, but they are usually there. Check to see what the expense ratio is for each fund you own. You will often find the expense ratio next to the balance in each fund. Take the expense ratio and multiply it by your ending balance to see what they are charging you. For example, if you have $10,000 in a fund with an expense ratio of 0.50 percent, you are paying $50 per year. Tally up all of your fund expenses to show your fees. What's reasonable? Around 1 percent or so. I have known of some cases where smaller plans will use a third party consultant or investment broker. By the time this middle person is paid, you could end up paying 2 percent or more. You may not notice this when the 401(k) is making money. When the cost is tacked onto losses, however — ouch!

## Missing Out on Free Money!

**Since many companies have stopped issuing pensions, and we are in do-it-yourself mode for our retirement security, one of the biggest mistakes is to not take full advantage of matching funds. If your employer is willing to match any contribution you make up to a percentage of your paycheck, by all means take that deal! It's like free money!**

**In some cases, the employer is willing to provide not only matching funds but profit-sharing contributions as well, usually based on a percentage of salary. Most employers match half of your contributions up to a maximum of 6 percent of your gross salary, but some match dollar-for-dollar, and for more than 6 percent. It varies from company to company and in some cases you have to stay on the job 10 years or so before you are fully vested in the extra contributions. Sadly, some fail to see the value of this and opt out entirely, only to regret such decisions later in life.**

## Rolling It Over Into an IRA

**Fortunately for us, 401(k) plans are portable. There are a few steps you will need to take to do it right, but your financial advisor should be able to walk you through the process. There will likely be forms to fill out that will instruct the custodian of the old plan to release the funds directly to your new custodian. It is often best to have the former plan administrator electronically transmit the value of the account to the new account. That is a direct rollover. When you get with your financial advisor, he or she should be able to walk you through the process and avoid any tax and penalty surprises that may otherwise result.**

[7]

# Predator #7 — Human Nature

**ONE OF THE best-loved comic strips of all time was Pogo, drawn by Walt Kelly until he died in 1973. The strip featured swamp dwellers Pogo Possum, Albert Alligator and other lovable cartoon animals through which Kelly projected his philosophy and political commentary. One of the most famous one-liners ever to come out of Pogo was, "We have met the enemy, and he is us." The frame depicted a disconsolate Pogo looking at a pile of trash and litter that had found its way to his remote swampland, making his home resemble a dump. The obvious message was that we humans are our own worst enemy sometimes.**

**We can be our own worst enemy when it comes to handling our finances. Take, for example, our tendency to procrastinate. At the beginning of this book I promised that we would not only point out many of the traps and pitfalls common to retirement, but also offer specific strategies and concepts that would steer you safely by them. I hope I kept that promise. In Chapter One we discussed the IRA tax time bomb. We explored the problems we could inadvertently create for our heirs by leaving them a lump sum, only to have as much as half of it gobbled up by the tax man. The solution?**

**Stretching the IRA. Taking advantage of perfectly legitimate provisions within the tax code that allow us to pass the proceeds of our IRA to our loved ones in such a manner that (a) it will grow over time to four times its original size and (b) we avoid the giant tax bite that would result otherwise.**

**This may or may not have applied to you. But I will bet my bottom dollar that some solutions presented in these pages will match a challenge you either are facing or will soon face if you are on the threshold of retirement. Does possessing knowledge of these strategies and solutions protect you? No, it does not. In the immortal words of American writer and lecturer Dale Carnegie, "Knowledge is not power until it is *applied.*"**

## Procrastination

**Procrastination, of course, is putting off until tomorrow what you should do today. Did you hear the one about the group of people who had such a problem with procrastination that they decided to start a support group? It never happened, however, because they kept putting it off.**

**But seriously, our human nature to procrastinate may be harmless when it comes to little things around the house, like organizing our sock drawer or cleaning out the garage, but it can cost us big time when it comes to handling our financial affairs. In Chapter Three we discussed the evils of probate and the chaos that can befall our loved ones should we pass away with our estate affairs in disarray. I cannot tell you how many people I have met in my line of work who, when we sit down to review their financial picture, don't even have a simple will. I preach against doing such things online, but even a fill-in-the-blanks will you can pick up at any office supply store is better than nothing at all.**

## Getting a Round "Tuit"

**Making an hour-long appointment with a financial advisor will probably cost you nothing. At our firm we do not charge a fee for the first appointment — what I call the "get acquainted" appointment — simply because that session is just to get to know each other and see if it is a mutual fit for us to work together. It may not be — in which case we hope to make a friend and move along. So that first appointment should be an easy one to make, shouldn't it? And yet, human nature being what it is, some slough it off as something they mean to do — and will do — when they get around to it.**

**I attended a seminar once where the featured speaker passed around a small, blue box to each person in attendance and told us not to open it until everyone had one. Naturally, we all wondered what was in the box and what could possibly be the point he was building up to. As he continued with his remarks, he gave several examples of how procrastination had cost individuals dearly.**

**The room fell silent when he told the story of a friend who had postponed getting a colonoscopy. The friend knew it was something he should attend to and kept telling himself he would — eventually — when he got around to it. Of course, the man never did and he died needlessly young of colon cancer.**

**Another story was the tragic tale of a family whose house burned down in a preventable fire because their smoke detectors had bad batteries. Replacing the batteries in the inoperative warning devices was on the homeowner's to-do list, but he just never got around to it. The fire claimed the lives of their twin daughters.**

**By this time, all of us in the room had almost forgotten about the box. Then the speaker told us we had in our hands the cure for procrastination and that we could now open the little blue box. Inside was a round wooden disc on which was printed in bold, black letters "TUIT." If we hadn't yet connected the wooden coin with the**

speaker's message, he made sure we go the point when he said, "If you have been procrastinating doing anything that needs doing in your life until you get around to it, you have no excuse now. You hold in your hands *a round tuit.* Now *do it.*"

## Procrastinating With Our Wealth

Almost as bad as procrastinating with our health is procrastinating with our wealth. One couple who made an appointment to meet with me following a financial workshop they had attended began our "get acquainted" session by telling me that I might not be able to help them. I asked them why. The man pointed to a grocery bag full of what appeared to be scrap paper and said, "Our personal financial life is a mess, and we don't know where to start."

In the bag were several envelopes, some open and many not, containing statements from various banks and investment accounts. The couple's net worth was well over $1 million. They owned a thriving business and were very successful at making money, but they weren't very good at keeping track of it. After we decided that we would work together, we set up another appointment, the objective of which was to plow into the paper bag and identify three things:

- How much they had
- Where it was
- What they wanted to do with it

As it turns out, these two people were in much better shape financially than either one of them had imagined, but they would have been in much better shape had they received some guidance over the past two decades. That was water over the dam, of course.

When we put all their accounts on a spreadsheet and went down the list, there was much consolidation that needed to be done, and in many of their accounts they were paying unnecessary fees because of duplicate mutual funds and scattered IRAs. Each year, their accountant would give them advice to pull money out of their cash flow and invest it, but the accountant gave them little direction as to how to invest the money. As a consequence, some of the accounts were earning little interest and others were going to cause tax problems down the road.

## Getting to Know the "Why"

Without a purpose, money is no more than numbers on a page or so much fancy paper. When I first sit down with new clients, I do most of the listening and they do most of the talking so that we can arrive at the purpose they have in mind for their wealth. It is crucial to understand the "why" before talking about the "how" and "what" of investing.

With this couple, for example, I wanted to know specifics about their vision of the future. Was there a specific target date for retirement? Did they want to travel? Or were they the type of individuals who would rather stay at home and play with the grandchildren? Maybe they wanted to do both. One couple who were two years away from retirement told me they wanted to take their grandchildren with them on a trip of their (the grandkids) choosing each year and just enjoy having fun with them. Maybe their plans for the future involved the beach, a second home, golf or a boat. Or it could be that these were the kind of people who were more interested in legacy — making sure their children and grandchildren were well cared for, financially. They could be charitably inclined. Or they could be like the people I saw recently on the highway, driving an expensive motor home with a sticker on the bumper that announced: "We are spending our children's inheritance." I had to know them on that level before I could begin to give them meaningful financial advice.

Everyone has a slightly different "why" to their financial picture. A competent financial professional will make no recommendations as to where to place assets for investment purposes until that "why" becomes clearly manifest in the interview process. As it turns out, this couple had a vision of the future unique to them. They had worked hard building their businesses, and they were proud of their accomplishments. Both their children were successful medical professionals had no interest in taking over the business. They envisioned working until they were 65, selling their business, and then doing some international traveling. The woman said that for years she had been collecting brochures of the Greek islands in the Mediterranean and the Holy Land, two places she had always wanted to visit. No one — at least no financial advisor — had ever asked them questions about such things. She said she felt relieved and more confident about the future now that her financial house had been put in order. The future was brighter and the road ahead easy to see.

"There was always this nagging voice in my head telling us we needed to do this," she said. "But we just kept putting it off."

Don't procrastinate on taking care of either your *health* or your *wealth.* I knew of one guy who would use any excuse to avoid seeing a doctor, even for his annual physical. He was healthy, too — ran three miles a day and ate lots of nuts and berries. I am writing about him in past tense because he is no longer with us. He started having abdominal pains and ignored them for a year or more, dosing up on pain killers. Finally, when the pain got the best of him, he caved in and went to the doctor to see what was wrong. By that time, the cancer that was inoperable. The doctors said his type of cancer would have been easy to deal with only six months earlier. His death could have been prevented.

Don't procrastinate on getting your financial house in order, either. It pains me to think of how many people are paying way too much in taxes. I cringe to think of how many have portfolios positioned for disaster when the next stock market crash arrives. I wince when I hear of individuals making poor decisions concerning Social Security, Medicare and long-term care insurance. Getting financial advice is painless and inexpensive compared to the alternative.

## Doing It Yourself

Independence can be a good thing, and there is nothing wrong with a do-it-yourself approach to many things. That having been said, I don't recommend self-surgery or self-dentistry. I know of individuals who choose to go it alone with their investing and financial planning, and some of them do OK. Unfortunately, there are many more stories that don't end well. I am not talking about those who like to do online stock trading with discretionary funds. This is a recreation for some individuals. One client of mine enjoys investing with what he calls his "play money." Even though his "play money" amounts to thousands of dollars, he still considers it money he can afford to lose. I'm not talking about that. My caution is directed at using your life savings — money you will need for your sunset years — to play the market. There is not much difference between that and going to Las Vegas and playing games of chance. Overall, financial management and income planning needs to be left to professionals. Why? Because our own human nature can become our enemy when emotions get in the way.

### Emotions Get in the Way

Investors who go it alone have a tendency to make decisions based on stock tips from friends, relatives and co-workers. When these hot stock tips don't work out, they have difficulty letting go. Remember the dot-com days of the 1990s? I had friends who loaded up on shares of start-up companies in those days because of the feeding frenzy. Anything that ended in dot-com was like a scratch-off lottery ticket guaranteed to be an instant winner. Some found it irresistible not to dump a few thousand dollars into those stocks with the anticipation that they could sit back and just watch the profits roll in. The profits did roll in for a while. Then the mood began to change on Wall Street. The trouble started with a little question mark. Could these stocks be overpriced? Could the exuberance of investors over companies who had no earnings history possibly be misguided? Was this just a bubble? As soon as those emotions (fear) began creeping into the picture, the dot-com boom was doomed. Some, however, wanted to believe this was just a little hiccup. It was normal for the market to retrace now and then, wasn't it? When tech stocks began inching down, emotions (greed) kept some investors holding on to wait for the big bounce upward to occur. When there was no bounce, emotions (panic) took over again, and fortunes were lost.

Professional money management is done without such emotions. Professional money managers use formulas, not hunches. Trusting your gut is OK in some circumstances, but few have the discipline to go about investing without emotions getting in the way at some point.

# [8]

# How to Choose the Right Advisor for YOU

> **"Never depend on a single income. Make investments to create a second source." ~ Warren Buffett**

**I HOPE I HAVE made the case for seeking professional help when it comes to managing your assets and planning your financial future in retirement. But that brings up the next question: How do you go about selecting the right financial advisor? How can you know which financial advisor is a good fit for you and your unique and special circumstances? You want someone who is knowledgeable, ethical, experienced and, perhaps most important, someone who will work with your best interest at heart and not their own. The truth is, not everyone calling himself or herself a "financial advisor" will meet those qualifications. Letters after someone's name on a business card do not necessarily mean that the person who had it printed should be trusted with your financial future. Neither does a fancy office building or plaques on an office wall. But there**

are specific things you can do to make sure you choose wisely in this area.

## Ask Lots of Questions

I like the interview process for this one. If you are going to place your trust, confidence and life savings in someone's hands, don't you think it is a good idea to know them both personally and professionally? I do. Real professionals will feel the same way. They will not mind your asking questions about their credentials and qualifications. They will welcome your inquiries. They will be happy to tell you about their training and the designations they have earned that represent their expertise and experience.

A competent, qualified professional will not take offense at this little interrogation. While they can't give you specifics, ask them for some generic examples of where they have helped people. If you were going to undergo an operation, would you rather have (a) a doctor who had performed the procedure thousands of times, or (b) a surgeon for whom you were their first operation? Option (a), of course! Trust is such a big factor in financial planning. You are going to select someone to guide you through one of the most crucial decision-making periods of your life. You want them to know what they are doing. Your life savings are probably involved. Assets you have worked hard all of your life to obtain. It is one thing to hang out a shingle that proclaims to the world that you are a "financial advisor." It is quite another to prove by evidence that you have spent years obtaining the required education it takes to render such advice accurately and effectively.

## Designations and Certifications

Here is the thing about designations and certifications. By themselves, they mean nothing. They infer knowledge, but you have to do your due diligence to see if that knowledge is there. When I hand people a business card, it is usually after we have spent some time together. They have gotten to know me, and I have gotten to know them. The men usually put the card in their shirt or coat pocket, and the women often put the card inside their purse. Rarely does anyone squint at the card and ask, "What does ChFC® mean?" It stands for Chartered Financial Consultant. I am happy to answer that question, as well as take them on a tour of all my plaques, certificates, degrees, etc. But that is not what they are interested in. They usually want to know if I have the experience, knowledge and competence to safeguard their assets and provide them with a good return on their money in retirement.

It reminds me of a story Zig Ziglar told about a man selling wood stoves. He told this story back in the days of the first oil crisis, when the price of heating oil went through the roof, and folks were buying wood-burning stoves as an alternative heating source. The stove salesman was talking to an elderly couple about all the features and benefits of the stove — the thickness of the iron, the quality of construction and the number of BTUs (British Thermal Units) it could put out. When he finished his spiel, he asked the couple if they had any questions, to which the woman replied, "Will it keep an old lady warm?" They could not have cared less about what a BTU was and how many the little stove could generate.

I am immediately suspicious when I see a business card or letterhead with a long string of letters after someone's name. The first thing I wonder is, "Why are they trying so hard to impress me with such things?" The main thing I'm interested in is what service they can perform for me and if we are a good fit for each other. To probe deeper into their qualifications and experience, the first question I usually ask is something like, "How did you get started in your profession?" In other words, tell me a little about yourself. Tell me how long you have been doing this. Why should I do business with you? What do you bring to the table? In other words, what service can you perform for me that will enhance my life, and how do I know you are genuinely interested in me and my welfare and have my best interests at heart and not your own? I am sure that I am not unlike you in this regard.

Don't get me wrong. Certification is important. But education and experience are more vital to the financial planning process.

## Ask Questions

Some questions to ask when you interview a financial advisor candidate are:

### How Are You Compensated?

This not a personal question. It may be considered rude and obnoxious to ask that question of someone you just met at a dinner party, but to ask it of a financial advisor is altogether appropriate. Why? Because it has a bearing on whether there may be conflicts of interest. It may reveal their level of objectivity. No financial professional I know works free of charge. If someone tells you that they do, I would look for the nearest exit door and doubt the next thing they say to you. Commissions and profit are what lubricate the gears of the American free enterprise system, and they are not dirty words. What you want is someone whose advice is not tainted or influenced by that.

## Are You a Fiduciary?

**Why ask them this? What is a fiduciary? It means the advisor has a fundamental obligation to act in the best interests of his/her clients and to provide investment advice in the clients' best interests. Fiduciaries owe their clients a duty of undivided loyalty and utmost good faith. They must employ reasonable care to avoid misleading clients and must provide full and fair disclosure of all material facts to clients and prospective clients. All possible conflicts of interest must also be disclosed.**

**If you are buying a car, any dealership you go to will try to sell you one of their automobiles. You don't expect the Ford dealer to laud the virtues, features and value of a Chevrolet. Car dealers are not fiduciaries. Car salesmen are not working in a fiduciary capacity. That doesn't mean they are trying to defraud you, but they are not obligated to take a universal approach to your automobile purchase. They are there to tell you all about their merchandise and influence you to buy it.**

**Neither is a stockbroker a fiduciary. Stockbrokers may work for a large brokerage house which has a limited menu of planning options for you, all of which (no big surprise here) involve your buying stocks or mutual funds from that company.**

**Fiduciaries are never under an obligation to recommend any one product or service. They are legally obligated to recommend what is best for their clients, period.**

**In the world of financial planning, advisors who are fiduciaries take the designation quite seriously and will not be offended if you ask them, "Are you a fiduciary?"**

## What Is Your Investing Philosophy?

**You will learn a lot from this question — more by what the candidate doesn't say than what the candidate does say. A true profes-**

sional will not answer the question in depth without first knowing what your goals, dreams, plans, aspirations, values, etc., are. It would be the same as asking a taxi driver, "Where are you headed?" That is the question the driver should be asking you!

You probably can't imagine a doctor prescribing medicine for you without first doing a thorough examination and finding out whether you are allergic to it. Neither would a true fiduciary make a recommendation to you without a full and thorough "financial examination."

Remember, there are accumulation specialists and distribution specialists. You know you are talking to an accumulation specialist if the answer to the above question starts with a list of stocks or mutual funds and focuses on their projected returns over the next 10 years or so. If you are approaching retirement, you may want to look elsewhere. It's a little like an adult soliciting medical advice from a pediatrician. In the medical community, the pediatrician would likely give you a referral — a courtesy that doesn't usually happen in the financial world.

## How Do You Work With Your Clients?

You ask this question to know if you will have regular reviews or if you will be left on your own. You should have at least an annual review of your financial plan to make sure that you are on track to meet your goals. Who is your contact person? Will you see the firm's principal only once in your lifetime and then be shuttled off to administrators? Or will the firm's principal take an active role in following through with your financial plan.

Regularly scheduled reviews are critical because tax rules change and the economic climate is ever-changing. Your life circumstances may change, also. You should expect at least an annual review.

## Other Qualifiers

### Does Your Advisor Candidate Understand Taxes and Insurance?

**Taxes can play a crucial role in financial planning. So can insurance. Some financial advisors aren't trained in either of these areas. When choosing an advisor, ask all the questions you know to ask about taxes and insurance, and then ask if there are any questions you forgot to ask. An advisor who is an expert in those areas will usually point out several you failed to mention. Fiduciary advisors will never "sell" insurance to their clients. On the other hand, they will be able to discern where there is a need for more insurance or if the clients are paying premiums for insurance they do not need.**

### Can They Help With Estate Planning?

**There is a lot more to estate planning than just having a will. True professionals will be able to provide strategies that will allow you to keep most of your family's wealth in the family and not in Uncle Sam's tax coffers. An advisor who specializes in estate planning will know where trusts may be useful. A competent financial advisor may have attorneys and other professionals as members of his or her extended team who will be able to execute any strategies that may be necessary for a fully comprehensive financial plan. That way, a complete review of your entire financial plan should require just one meeting in one office.**

### Are They Independent?

**This is a very important question. In other words, does he or she work for a company? If they are there to sell you products instead of providing strategies, you will know it after a few of these questions. The work they do for you needs to be solely for you and customized to your unique circumstances. Some financial advisors have what I**

call a "menu." Choose Plan A, B or C — as if one of those ought to fit you. No. You are uniquely you, and your financial picture is individual. There is no cookie-cutter solution. Nothing out of the one-size-fits-all bin is acceptable.

You will find that most stockbrokers work for broker-dealers and, as the term "broker" suggests, they are there to put the investor together with the investment company. Most brokers work under a suitability standard, not the fiduciary standard. The fiduciary standard puts the advisor on the level of problem-solving, not product-selling.

## The Golden Rule

"Do unto others as you would have them do unto you," reads the Golden Rule. I wouldn't want to be charged a fee just to have a "look-see" to determine if I and a financial advisor candidate were a good fit for each other. I have had people come in and tell me that they already have a financial advisor (we will call him Bob) and that they have known Bob for a long time, and they trust him. I have nothing but admiration for that kind of loyalty. Sometimes they just want a second opinion — a move I think is wise. No true professional will oppose their clients obtaining a second opinion. In the medical profession, it is almost expected that before you commit to a serious operation (to me, any operation is serious) you obtain a second opinion from another qualified medical professional. Most doctors will even provide references for second opinions if you ask them.

The Golden Rule also dictates that I follow the Chartered Life Underwriter's Pledge, which is to recommend to my clients only what I would apply to myself. It may sound corny to say I truly care about the people I am helping, but I really do — from the bottom of my heart. After I thoroughly understand a client's financial situation, I am confident in the advice I give them — so confident, in fact, that I would not hesitate to offer identical advice to a family member or apply the advice to myself.

When we conduct the "get acquainted" interview, and I ask someone what he or she does for a living, I will get any number of interesting responses. I am always intrigued at just how many professions and occupations there are out there in this big, wide world. I have also observed that, even though we are all different in so many respects, we are all much the same when it comes to our dreams, goals and aspirations.

## Taking Action Is Required

Thank you for taking the time to read my book. I hope you enjoyed reading it as much as I enjoyed writing it for you. And I hope you found some of the contents useful to you in preparing for your financial future. If that is the case, I would love to say, "Mission accomplished!" but it wouldn't be the truth. The truth is all the knowledge in the world doesn't help us unless we apply it. If I have said that too many times in this book, I apologize. It's just that it is oh, so true.

While attending a continuing education seminar a few years back, I heard the speaker give an unforgettable illustration regarding the difference between knowledge, understanding and wisdom. If you are standing in the middle of the road and you see a bus barreling toward you, that is knowledge. Understanding is discerning the relationship between your somewhat frail makeup compared with a hard metal object, a.k.a. the bus, which is coming right at you. Wisdom is getting out of the way.

If any of the strategies or concepts introduced to you here have merit and could improve the quality of your retirement, you owe it to yourself to examine them and see if they fit your circumstances. I

**would consider it an honor and a privilege to meet you face-to-face and answer personally any questions you may have about anything you have read here. My contact information can be found on the back cover of the book.**

# Afterword

**My inspiration for writing this book came from my growing concern that many of my fellow baby boomers may be falling substantially short of the mark when it comes to preparing themselves for retirement. It is my hope that this book will inform readers of the steps needed to ensure successful retirement and encourage them to take those steps. Because of our country's ever-changing economic landscape, I believe there has never been a more critical time for those of our unique generation to make sure the financial pathway they are on is one that will lead to their financial independence.**

**For all of you who bought my book and are reading it, I personally wish to commend you for seeking to educate yourself on this often complex topic. I encourage you to remain diligent in your quest for knowledge. The decisions you make with regard to your retirement and your investments will most likely be the most important financial decisions you will ever make.**

# Acknowledgments

**This book would have not been possible without the tremendous support of my current staff members, Vicki Zimmerman, Jennifer Delcolmyn, Peggy Mott, Brooke Reynolds and former staff member Judy Gossett, who served as my office manager for 19 years; my son, best friend and business partner, Colin Evans, who was a tremendous help in rereading my copy and helping me edit the book. Thanks also to my wife, Gale, who has supported me now for 45 years and counting. She has always understood my passion for helping people and has accepted both my calling and the demanding schedule that goes along with it. It goes without saying what an invaluable assistance this has been. Without her, I could not have written this book.**

**I also want to personally thank my friend and copy editor, Tom Bowen, whose patience and encouragement kept the project going. He piloted my thoughts and wisdom on this important information and was a true catalyst in the production of this book.**

**Most importantly I want to thank my Lord and Savior who has blessed me with the gift of being able to help people obtain financial independence, something that continues to give me immeasurable satisfaction in my life. He has also surrounded me with extraordinary people in my workplace, which makes my job a true joy every day. Through Him all things are possible, and we must never forget to thank Him each day for the countless blessings He bestows upon each and every one of us.**

# Acknowledgments

[illegible]

## ABOUT THE AUTHOR

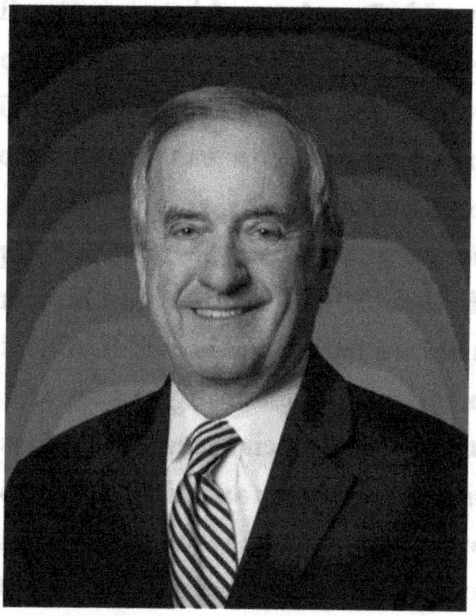

**David Evans grew up in Williamstown, New Jersey. He and his wife, Gale, now live in Shreveport, Louisiana, where Dave is president of Evans Financial Group, a full-service financial planning firm he founded in 1988. He is an Investment Advisor Representative of Brookstone Capital Management, a Registered Investment Advisor.**

Dave and Gale met at a high school dance and were married Aug. 23, 1969. They have a son, Colin, who joined the firm in 2000 and now works with his father at Evans Financial Group as a managing partner and Certified Annuity Specialist. Colin, Dave and Gale attend The Church at Red River.

Dave graduated from Lamar University in Beaumont, Texas, in 1972 with a degree in marketing. He is a Chartered Life Underwriter (CLU) and a Chartered Financial Consultant (ChFC). Dave is a "Top of the Table" member of the Million Dollar Round Table, an elite designation that represents the top 1 percent of all financial advisors in the world. Dave began his career as a financial professional in 1973 working for MONY (Mutual of New York) and became securities licensed in 1976. He quickly rose through the ranks and became a sales manager and then was promoted to the company's home office where he worked as an assistant to the director of training. He moved to Louisiana in 1980 to accept a position as manager of a Shreveport office, a position he would hold for the next eight years before founding his own financial firm. Dave began focusing on retirement planning in 2003 and has forged the firm into a multifaceted financial services business with multiple investing and asset preservation and distribution tools.

"I consider our main mission is to alleviate financial worry by preparing our clients for what's coming next," Dave says. "We want to arm them with strategies that help them reach their financial goals without exposing them to unnecessary risk."

The five staff members of Evans Financial have a combined 75 years of experience in wealth management and take pride in helping those on the threshold of retirement and those already in retirement reach their financial goals.

"We don't have a template for our clients, and we don't have tiers of agents that work with only well-heeled clients," Dave says. "Each of our clients gets personalized service with a creative approach to financial planning and money management. Our mission is to empower our clients to make their own decisions."

According to Dave, it's not the product that produces optimal results, it's the process and the strategies used to make it work. He says the prime directive at Evans Financial is its focus on people and placing the goals of clients above all else.

"People don't care how much you know until they know how much you care," Dave says.